A NEW DAWN IS BREAKING

Independents Now Have a Voice in Washington

BY: J. DAVID POLING, SR.

A New Dawn is Breaking

jdpolingsr@cox.net

Copyright 2017 by J. David Poling, Sr.

All rights reserved

Printed and bound in the United States of America

First printing, August 14, 2017 by Moore Graphics, Youngtown, AZ

Book Cover by Don Mulkey of Mill Valley, CA and Moore Graphics.

This book is published by The Wildcat Publishing Group in conjunction with the author, J. David Poling, Sr.

Copyright Applied for: August 15, 2017

Other Books by this Author

*****

What a Great Ride It Has Been!

The Story of My Life

*****

The Inner Circle,

A Modern Political Novel

*****

Your Life Is

Really Worth Writing About

This book is dedicated to:

All of the people in the United States who are waiting patiently for a return to clear thinking and some degree of honest and sane professionalism in all of our legislative bodies: from the City Halls to the State Capitals, to the House of Representatives, the Senate and most especially to the White House.

Foreword

I began writing a novel about Presidential politics in 2009, and the result was my first novel, *The Inner Circle, a Modern Political Novel*, which dealt with my strong feelings about the existing political parties, but in particular my unhappiness with my own party - The Republican Party. In that novel, a 3rd party is born and its candidate Mark Worthington receives a preponderance of the popular votes, and in the end is poised to become the next President of the United States.

Now, I don't know about other writers of fiction, novels in particular, but in my case I found myself involved in several projects, important to me, but not to my writing! So, before I knew it, it was 2016 and we were faced with another Presidential election in this country. I honestly believe that this was one of the most important elections in our history. The campaign was almost without precedent, and the two candidates who finally remained standing were both flawed at best. Without elaborating too much, I can assure my readers that I am no less dissatisfied with my party, the Republicans and their choice for President, than I was six years ago, nor am I any happier with the Democrats and their choice. I think the country was dealt a very bad hand to play, and after a few months under the new President, nothing has happened to make me feel more comfortable.

Thus I decided it was time to return to the 'fantasy land' of the novel where a genuine white knight emerges to hopefully lead the country "out of the wilderness."

However, I now see this effort becoming a Trilogy where eventually the author will be able to deal with governing issues - something neither of the current political parties seems to be very good at.

May 12, 2017

Introduction

My 2010 book *The Inner Circle, a Modern Political Novel*, dealt with the reality that political parties have been rapidly growing more polarized as the country entered the 21st century. The Democrats were more and more being labeled as the uncontrollable liberals and the Republicans were accused of being dominated by the ultra-conservative economic theorists, all too often tied hand in glove with the Christian right.

Finally in the recently completed primary season the Democrats, true to form, nominated their incumbent President who had only a few weeks before moved into the Presidency upon the untimely death of their young and charismatic President. But there were a great many Democrats who were very disgruntled by this outcome.

The President had been a long time Senator before finally being nominated as a Vice Presidential candidate. He was a "safe" plodding candidate who had complemented the young and relatively unknown Presidential candidate. But once he moved into the oval office he felt he had to stamp his presence on all aspects of the office. He replaced nearly all of the holdovers from the former President's circle and he did it in very short order.

The new President was a very impatient person who believed without any trace of doubt that he was ordained to become President at some time in his life. The fact that he had entered numerous primaries in many different Presidential campaigns and was uniformly rejected by the Democratic Party meant very little to him. The political leader he admired the most was Lyndon Johnson, and wheeling and dealing, cajoling and threatening were all part of his political makeup. He was a relatively small man with a large and often menacing voice. It didn't take too much to set him off and when any one of his staff, advisors, elected officials or the press had the temerity to use the term 'accidental President'. He would explode in a thunder of crude and acerbic comments generally ending with "you're fired!"

****

The Republicans battled through what seemed like an endless number of primaries and a succession of debates with the Governor of Texas, representing the traditional conservative side of the party finally emerging as their Candidate. But, Bobby Drew Houston was not to be anointed by all Republicans, a great many of whom supported the very moderate candidacy of former General Mark Worthington.

Houston closely fit the caricature of a Texas politician who had bullied his way to the top of the party in the Lone Star State, and who also admired the political acuity of LBJ. He was tall and ruggedly good looking, but a very shallow thinker on most topics outside the state of Texas. He committed numerous gaffes on the campaign trail but managed to please the religious right and the deeply conservative tea party side of the party.

Houston was homophobic and very close to being an anti-feminist, particularly with the way he dealt with the primary candidacy of Senator Ellen Livingston. But through some backroom wheeling and dealing he had managed to persuade one of the other leading candidates, ex-Governor Jimmy

Foxworthy to give up his quest and hand over the large number of delegates he had already acquired to the Houston total. That was enough to put him over the top and for that boost Houston named Foxworthy to be his running mate.

****

General Mark Worthington was a recently retired 4 Star General who had held major military campaign and theater responsibilities in the Middle East, Europe and finally as Chief of Staff of the Joint Chiefs in Washington. He was a graduate of West Point, first in his class, later earning a Masters and a Ph.D. in International Affairs. He and his wife retired to a quiet and comfortable life teaching at the University of Illinois in Champagne, Illinois.

Mark Worthington was of moderate height and weight, but extremely svelte with the bearing always associated with great military figures. However he was modest and thoughtful and always sought advice where he felt unsure of the political minefields he faced during the primaries. But he also was dynamic as a speaker generally speaking without notes, in a quiet but firm voice. He commanded the attention of his listeners because of the trust they automatically seemed to feel in his presence. He was not a spellbinding speaker but one who quickly gained the rapt attention of his listeners who wanted to hear more of his reasoned and hopeful messages.

Gordon Metcalfe, a long time and highly regarded former Republican Party Chairman, eventually convinced Mark Worthington to enter the Republican Party Primary campaign and then later to take the even bigger step up to becoming a third party candidate; and for the first time since the days of Ross Perot, the country found itself with a legitimate alternative to either of the polarized major parties. Because Mark Worthington's candidacy was so highly regarded a great many Congressmen and women chose to switch their party allegiance to his newly formed Independence Party even before the election.

The result of all this dramatic maneuvering was electric! Mark Worthington ran well ahead of both the President and Bobby Drew Houston in the popular vote count, and at midnight of election night he was within just a few electoral votes of clinching the election outright. But at that late hour there was still some uncertainty as to the final outcome………

The list of characters who have already played major roles in this story:

General Mark Worthington, Retired four star General and Independence Party Candidate for President

The President of the United States and Democratic candidate for President

Sen. Jaime Gonzalez (FL) and Republican VP candidate

Gov. Bobby Drew Houston (Texas) the Republican candidate for President

Jimmy Foxworthy ex-Gov of Arkansas and Republican Vice Presidential candidate

Sen. Ellen Livingston (NJ)

Sen. Robert Madison (WI)

Gordon Metcalfe, Independence Party Chairman (formerly Chairman of the RNC)

Bryce Randolph, retired Consultant and member of the Worthington's campaign Inner Circle

Senator Jeff Corcoran (Ohio)

Rep. Steve Marsh (MI)

Gov. Earl Potts (Iowa)

Ernie Hardesty, Sen elect from Iowa

Charlie Wipperman, Iowa businessman and Republican Elector

Wally Backstrom, Chairman of the DNC

Chapter 1

The Morning after the Presidential Election

Mark Worthington had gone to bed on Election Night fairly certain that he was no longer either 'General' or 'Candidate' Mark Worthington, but that he would now be known only as President-elect Mark Worthington. It had been around 1:00am when CBS reluctantly conceded that the election had been a stunning upset and it now appeared that Mark Worthington, the third party candidate of the Independence Party appeared to have enough electoral votes to win the election outright.

So, after many congratulatory phone calls, he and Janet finally fell asleep around 3:30am. Mark woke up about 6:30 (way past his normal rising hour) made some coffee and woke his wife. They quietly joked about the fact that they would be making still another move in their married life. But what a move! To the White House no less! As they sipped their coffee he reached over and clicked the TV monitor to see what Greg Putnam, the morning anchor-person on CBS, had to say. Mark was scheduled to meet with his transition team at 9:00 am but he was more than a little curious just how close the final results were going to be.

To his utter shock, he heard Putnam's dulcet tones reveal "It appears that everyone was a bit hasty last night in 'crowning' Mark Worthington as our next President. Although it does appear that he has been given a substantial popular vote lead, the electoral college is still up in the air. Hundreds of thousands of votes from Illinois, Texas and Maryland are still being counted and the results appear to be too close to make a definitive call in any of those three states."

The anchorman continued "The Republican National Committee is screaming loud and long, that the 'ever corrupt' Chicago political machine' is delaying the vote in and around Cook County, and they are alleging that a gigantic ballot box fraud is in the process of being carried out right now 'under our very noses' in an effort to steal enough votes to throw Illinois into the President's column which might very likely deny Worthington the needed electoral votes to claim the Presidency outright."

With that said, the morning host turned to a rather bleary eyed Roger, the inimitable talking head who had been up all night, and said "what do you make of these accusations Roger?"

"Well, Chicago does have a rather long, and somewhat sordid history as far as dragging out the vote counting, and I guess if I was in the shoes of Bobby Houston and the Republican party I'd be pretty suspicious too."

"Well, then what about the results out of Texas? That seems to be a real close vote too."

"Yeah, that's also pretty interesting. It sure appears that they are taking their good old time counting the million or more absentee ballots. And just so we don't show any favoritism here the Democratic National Committee is screaming that Bobby Houston who of course just *happens* to be the Governor of Texas may be in the process of pulling a "Lyndon Johnson" down there by trying to rig the results so that the Republicans take Texas which – again - would probably keep Worthington from getting the electoral votes he needs to nail down the election right now."

"And then…..?"

"If he should lose both of those states the election would be forced into the House of Representatives to decide."

"Okay, so what do you think about Maryland?"

"Well, here's what it looks like to me. Maryland is usually a pretty solid blue state – Democratic all the way. But this year there was an unusually large number of absentee ballots cast. As a matter of fact, almost twice as many as usual, so they're slowly working out from under the pile and who knows how that might turn out! But at least no one seems to pointing fingers and yelling fraud with that one!"

"It looks like Worthington has a modest lead with the votes cast at the polls, but perhaps this pile they are working on could swing the vote to one of the other two. Is that what the people in Annapolis are thinking?"

"That's it exactly. But as interesting and intriguing as the conspiracy talk surrounding Chicago and Austin, the truth of the matter is they too have a very large number of absentee ballots to count. It seems to me that no one really considered the possibility that thousands, perhaps hundreds of thousands, of independent voters might have decided to vote early.

"Interesting, indeed. But meanwhile, we don't yet have a clear cut winner. When do you think we'll know?"

"Well, my guess would be possibly Thursday afternoon, but it could also go into Friday or the weekend as well. They are pulling out all the stops in those three capitols, so I think we should start getting some official results at least by Monday."

Chapter 2

There had been a large crowd milling around the Democratic National Committee (DNC) headquarters all night long. Along about 11 o'clock on Election Night a good many of the faithful, both volunteer and paid alike had drifted away when the results showed the President trailing far behind both Bobby Houston and Mark Worthington.

The Chairman of the DNC had a secure line in his office available only to the White House where the President and his immediate political advisors had been huddled all evening long, even well after midnight. About 4 o'clock in the morning they began to see that they just might have a chance to throw this election into the House if one or two big states should swing into their column.

When the White House phone rang, the DNC chairman, Wally Backstrom, quickly grabbed it and said, "Backstrom here." He fully expected to hear one of the President's campaign advisors asking him if he had heard about what was going on in Illinois and Texas. He really didn't like any of the crew that the new President had gathered around him in the past few weeks. The new Chief had summarily rid himself of the people who were the political backbone of the former President within just a very few weeks of the President's death, and Wally thought it was a disastrous move, because most of these new guys had precious little experience in Washington and they tended to be toadies around the new President. He frankly wondered how he had managed to survive the blood bath administered by the new President – but then he figured if they lost this election, as it appeared they were about to do, then he, too, would probably be looking for work on January 20th, if not sooner.

But to his surprise, it wasn't a toady, but it was the President himself roaring into the microphone "Goddamn it, we still have a chance to get this thing into the House, Backstrom! So what are you doing to make that happen?"

Backstrom barely had a chance to acknowledge the question, when the President screamed at him again, "I'll tell you what you are going to do. Call that damn son of a bitch, the Mayor of Chicago, and tell him if he wants to have even a prayer of getting elected to a second term he better call in all the chips! I want Illinois and those electoral votes!"

Backstrom held the phone away from his ear as the President continued his raving. He then responded in as cool a voice as he could possibly muster "I'll call the mayor, but I have to tell you I'm not at all sure that there is much he can do to change the results. Things just aren't like they used to be under old man Daley."

The President fired back "You know I should have fired you when I got rid of all those ass-holes who were practically all from Chicago. I don't know what possessed me to hang on to you, you worthless piece of shit. So, are you going to get that slimy Mayor to fix things in Chicago or not?"

Backstrom took a very deep breath, drawing on all of the professional skill he had accumulated over some forty years in politics, and replied "I will call the Mayor, and do the best I can to deliver Illinois Mr. President."

Before Wally Backstrom did anything else, he pushed a button on his phone and listened to the conversation he had just had with the President of the United States. He quickly inserted a CD and made a copy of the conversation and put the copy in his brief case.

The President didn't bother to respond but merely reached over and hit the cut-off button. He turned to the six men who were sitting around his desk in the oval office and said, "Can you believe we have that no account bastard as our National Chairman. Here I am, a sitting President, popular with Democrats and Independents both, and he can't do any better than bring me in third? THIRD! Can you believe that? THIRD! I can't believe that I didn't win this thing outright! Well, I'll tell you what, if he doesn't deliver Illinois this week, he'll be looking for a job next Monday. I'm sick and tired of his 'can't do this, can't do that' attitude!"

With that the President slumped back into his chair. All of the others in the room except one mumbled a few words of agreement and encouragement. But Jeremiah Brady who was in charge of the White House's own polling organization spoke up with some trepidation. "Mr. President, at the risk of making you even angrier, I think it is only fair to Mr. Backstrom to note that the polls over the last 4-5 weeks consistently showed your popularity in the low 20% range......."

He didn't anymore get the words out of his mouth when the President leaped to his feet and came whipping around the corner of his desk where Brady was sitting. First the President balled up his fists and then grabbed Brady's coat collar and drew him up right out of his chair, and said "And you too, Brady. I suppose now you are going to refer to me as 'the accidental President? You're as bad as Backstrom. Who ever taught you how to do political polling? You all know that figures like that are a bunch of crap. I am one of the most popular Presidents this country has ever had, and I can't understand who the hell your so-called experts were talking to. Who did you call, were they all from a list of Republican political donors? I don't need you either. You're fired! Get the hell out of here! I want your desk cleaned out before 8 o'clock this morning and I don't ever want to see you or any of your incompetent staff around here after today. Get out!"

Brady reached down and picked up his brief case, and quickly exited the Oval Office. The President returned to his chair and muttered "Another piece of shit that we're better off without.'

This time there was total silence among the remaining five men in the room.

Chapter 3

Jamie Gonzalez, the Junior Senator from Florida, went to bed election night clearly believing that on Wednesday the world would begin addressing him as Mr. Vice-President-elect, or some such title. Whatever? He thought to himself.

He and his wife Cissy were in a suite on the other side of the same floor with Mark Worthington and Janet. Their year old daughter was in Illinois with Cissy's parents. It had been decided that having them on the same floor would make it a whole lot easier for the Secret Service to watch over both of them. They had fallen in bed about 2:45 am and as much as both of them really wanted to enjoy making love that night, they were simply too exhausted and almost immediately fell asleep in each others arms.

Jamie knew that he had to be at a command performance meeting at 9 in Mark's conference room, so he set the alarm on the night stand to come on with some light music about 6:30. It didn't take much noise to wake him out of a sound sleep so he quickly turned the radio off and slipped into the bathroom. He looked in the mirror and thought "a few more hours of sleep would have been really good for you sonny-boy!" But then he also thought Hell, the rest of the team can't be looking much better, now can they?

He slipped out of his pajamas and after warming the shower for a couple of minutes he stepped into the nice warm water. He liked the soap in most of these hotels because he could get a lot of lather up quickly and he covered himself in soap just before he felt a rush of cold air enter the shower. No sooner than he felt the cool air, the sliding door shut and it was warm again. Cissy was in the shower behind him hugging him from behind. "You didn't think you were going to sneak off this morning without a little hugging from your ever-lovin', now did you?" as she proceeded to help him a little with his application of the soap.

He turned and embraced her as they both stood in the shower enjoying each other's presence. Finally, she pushed back and reaching up took his head in her hands and gave him a long, sensuous kiss. "That is the first kiss the new Vice President of the United States is getting on the day after his election," she whispered in his ear. With that she left the shower as quickly as she had entered leaving Jamie to shampoo his hair.

When he stepped out of the shower area she was all ready to follow him in and finish her shower. He looked at her with total admiration for how well she had kept her figure after the baby was born, and he thought just how much he loved her.

They had ordered a light continental breakfast and after the bus boy had left, they sat for a minute and talked seriously about what a momentous occasion yesterday was – not just for them, certainly, but for the country as a whole.

"You know" she said, "I've been a political reporter my whole adult life, and you would think that I would be an old hand at this sort of thing. But what happened yesterday was …..was…..*seismic*! Almost nothing in our history approaches what you guys pulled off. It's…it's just wonderful, it's unbelievable, but you know what Jamie? It's also really scary, really, really scary! Who knows how you and your happy little band of warriors are going to be able to govern? Boy, I just can't wait to see how things develop. It is going to be *so* exciting!"

Jamie sat opposite her with a big smile on his face as he watched her very expressive face and her beautiful big brown eyes as she told him how excited she was: for them, and for the whole country. "I woke up this morning with the same thoughts going through my head. We are on the very edge of what is going to be one of the most important four years in our country's history. Think of it! We will be governing here almost like England governs their country. Three parties, all with very different agendas, all trying to get popular support, all trying to get their agenda through, at the same time knowing that they now have to compromise and be sensitive to the other two for a change.

"And I'm going to be sitting up there in the driver's seat in the Senate, holding the gavel and the all important tie breaking vote that you just know is going to be important – big time important! I just pray to God that Mark and I are up to it. It is going to be so different!"

"She reached over and placed both of her hands on his and very quietly offered "My love, you and Mark are the perfect pair to be steering this ship. The country just could not have picked two people with as much political smarts coupled with tons of integrity like you two. Yeah, you will do just fine. I know you will! Now get out of here and go down and meet with your leader! And give him a kiss for me. Well, on the other hand maybe you shouldn't give him a kiss!"

Laughing at what she had just said she stood and gave him a big hug and another long loving kiss and whispered in his ear, "I am so proud of you!"

Chapter 4

Mark Worthington strode into the concierge floor meeting room that the Hotel had provided and noted that all of the smiling, happy faces from the night before had become rather grim, as they all anxiously watched the various political commentators intoning on the surprising overnight developments.

"Good morning everyone! Hope some of you got at least a little bit of sleep last night."

"Good morning Mr. President" was said by just about everyone in the room.

"Whoa, not so fast folks. It sounds like there may still be a bump or two in the road. Cody, what do you hear on that wonderful grapevine of yours?"

Cody Templeton was recruited to join the Worthington team by California Congressman Mitchell Briggs. He was a young, twenty something media geek who had cut his political teeth in California. He was into every bit of new technology available. He worked the internet, blog sites, twitter, Facebook, town meetings and press conferences. He could and did it all.

"It's a mixed bag sir." With that he moved to an easel that was set up in the corner of the room with a white pad. He took out a black marking pen and began to write on the pad.

"Here is what we know for sure. (Cody wrote and talked at the same time:

1. ***You won the popular vote***
   (by a substantial margin over both the President and
   Bobby Houston.)

2. ***close to 141,000,000 votes cast***
   (which is a whopper of a turnout,)

3. ***Worthington 44% or 62,000,000***;

4. ***Houston and the Republicans got 29% or
   41,000,000,***

5. ***President and the Democrats got about 27% or
   38,000,000***

6. ***Electoral votes without Illinois, Texas and
   Maryland*** currently stands at:

   - ***Worthington: 253***

   - ***Houston: 189***

   - ***The President: 31***

   - ***Needed to win outright: 270***

   - ***Illinois 20, Maryland 9 and Texas 36
     are not final***

Gordon Metcalfe who nearly a year before had left the
Republican Party as National Chairman, just before they were
getting ready to fire him, had recruited Mark Worthington to
run for President as a Republican, and then later as a late entry
third party candidate. He then managed a brilliant campaign for
the candidate, as the results just put on the board demonstrated.

Gordon nodded toward Cody "Nicely done Cody – right to the point. We take either Illinois or Texas and we win outright. If we fail to take one of those two states then the election will be thrown into the House of Representatives to select the new President. Simple as that!"

Mark directed his comments to Gordon "What chance do we have to win in the House – if it should get that far?"

Gordon Metcalfe had been a powerful force in the Republican Party for most of his adult life. He rose to the top of the Party and was considered by nearly all of the 'political experts' to be the consummate political operative. He had done it all and done it well. The moment of truth came when he finally recognized the perilous course that the far right of his party was taking. He finally decided to challenge the Party to change its ways, and he lost. But the GOP's loss was Mark Worthington's gain. So, as always, Gordon was careful to gather his thoughts before he spoke.

Gordon finally responded "probably not a very good chance at all. Each state delegation in the House sits down and votes on the three candidates who got electoral votes. A majority vote of the state delegation decides who gets that state's votes. Unfortunately, because we started up your Independence Party third party campaign so late in the game we are in a decided minority in every single state delegation. A lot of the Representatives are leaning our way but most of them owe their positions and a lot of their financial support to either the Democrats or the Republicans. So they'll tend to vote with their party which leaves us out in the cold."

"So our big hope is for at least one of these two big states to go for us – is that it?"

"That's it!"

"'Okay, so did we actually win any seats in Congress outright – either House?"

Joe Bonafacio immediately took that question. "Yes sir, it certainly looks like we did pretty damn well considering the long odds against us. What with the candidates who switched parties to join us and the people we were able to recruit to run at the last minute, it looks like we may end up with as many as 60 to 70 Independence Party Congressmen and maybe 8 to as many as 12 Senators."

Gordon smiled a big Metcalfe smile and he said, "Not bad at all, especially, as you say, considering the odds we had to overcome. If we play our cards right we may just get a majority by the time the next Presidential election is held."

Mark Worthington set his coffee cup down and said "That sure sounds good to me, too. But Gordon what do you think those other guys are doing right now? They certainly aren't sleeping in this morning figuring it's all over, are they?"

"Well, my guess is that the electric bill at the White House will be considerably higher this month with what was probably an all-nighter in the Oval Office. My guess is they are going to pull every string they can to get enough votes to win in Illinois. We all know that Dick Daley won the election for JFK in 1960 with whatever shenanigans he pulled off, but I really have trouble believing that they can do that again. The new Mayor there sure doesn't have any warm spot in his heart for the President – not after he purged all of his old cronies right after the other guy died. So I just don't know what they can do, but that doesn't mean they can't try.

"I do think that we need to keep a close eye on Texas however. Bobby is the Governor there and he is as ruthless as they come. If there is a way to steal that state's votes he'll find it!"

Cody interjected, "Do you think either George H.W. or Junior would want to be a part of some kind of vote grab like LBJ pulled off way back when? It just doesn't sound like the way they operate."

Gordon replied, "Yeah, I agree with you Cody – but only to a point. They both figured out how to get elected – three times at that – and the 2000 Florida ballot fiasco wasn't exactly pretty. But, I think the bigger issue down south this year is whether they want to see Bobby Houston have a chance at getting elected. They were both awfully quiet throughout the whole campaign – which tells me they don't much give a damn whether he wins or not."

Cody spoke up again and said "I have a lot of people watching things in all three of these states, and also over at the RNC and the DNC. As a matter of fact, I just got a tweet that is interesting. One of my friends sent me a message a few minutes ago that says Jeremiah Brady just got handed his head this morning in a meeting at the Oval Office. What the hell do you suppose that's all about?"

Gordon let out a very low whistle and answered "Well, I would say that the President probably never liked Brady anyhow, and I'm sure he suspects that Brady doesn't much care for him either. Maybe he blames Jerry for their poor showing. You know that is a pretty big ego sitting behind the big desk there at 1600.Then again, maybe the President didn't want to believe the poll numbers which showed him running a very poor third for a full month before the election."

"Yeah" Joe Bonafacio chimed in," and Brady is from Chicago and one of the few holdovers from the old guy's team."

Gordon kind of summed it up with "My guess is that if the election doesn't get thrown into the House, then Wally Backstrom will be out of a job in a few days also."

Mark looked around the room and in a very measured tone of voice said, "This has been a good session and I don't want to drag it out."

Mark turned to Paul Matthews, his Press Secretary and said "Paul, start thinking about what our official response will be in either case, 'win outright' or 'into the House." Sketch out what our position will be and get back to me in a few hours so that I can have a chance to look at it. Okay?"

Paul nodded okay, and Mark then followed with "Let's get together again about 4 this afternoon and see if there has been any change in the picture. See you all then."

Chapter 5

Christopher John Black had been a feature writer for nearly 15 years and as he sat at his breakfast table looking at the Chicago Tribune he was suddenly consumed by an idea that had been just below the conscious level in his mind for several weeks. Mark Worthington, one of the foremost American generals in recent history, was right on the cusp of being elected President. It had been only a few months since he had been just another retired General teaching a class in Geo-politics at the University of Illinois at Champaign.

He looked over at his wife Cyndy and ventured "How the hell did he ever manage to pull this thing off?"

She was reading the business section of the paper and she looked up and said "How the hell did who manage to do what?"

Chris put the paper down and said "Mark Worthington! How did he ever manage to get this close to the Presidency from where he was a year ago? I know he's one bright guy, but who were the guys that put all of this together. He didn't do this all by his lonesome!"

"No, of course not. He had to have some really smart, capable people advising him along the way. If you really want to know who the players were that put this whole thing together, why don't you call Cissy Gordon and ask her. I really should say Cissy Gonzalez now that she's married to Jamie Gonzalez. She'll know who all of the players are. He *is* going to be the next Vice President you know!"

"Well, maybe he will and maybe he won't. It all depends on this damn electoral college thing. But, you are absolutely right. Cissy would certainly be able to fill me in on the grisly details."

"I'll tell you what Chris. I should call Cissy anyway and congratulate her on her husband's win, and I'll see if she would be willing to sit with you for an hour or two and let you in on some of the inside stuff of their campaign. I'm sure she could find the time to do that for an old J-School classmate! But what is it exactly that you want to write about."

"Well, here's what's bugging me. There was a guy named Theodore White who wrote a bunch of books all called something like **The Making of the President** but about different elections. He wrote one about John F. Kennedy winning in 1960 that became a real classic because that race was so close. So, I'm looking at this election and its even closer than 1960, *and* we have a third party maybe going to win it all.

"It just strikes me as being so damn unique in our history, that somebody needs to try and capture the whole picture. Just think about what has happened this year At the start of the year we had this charismatic young President who was in a good position to win a second term and then the unthinkable happens and just before the Democratic Convention he has a heart attack and dies.

"This left the Vice President taking over the Presidency and along with that the control of the Party. So the odds which were at worst even up on the President's chance for re-election now are tilted heavily away from the incoming Vice President. "

"I think I see where you are going, but isn't what's so unusual about the whole thing is what happened to the Republicans, not the Democrats?"

"Yeah, exactly! The two favorites for the Republicans, the Governor of Texas and the retired Governor of Arkansas were beating each other up really good and hardly paying any attention to the rest of the other wanna bes: when all of a sudden out of nowhere comes this guy on a white horse and he comes within a hairs breadth of winning the Republican nomination.

"But if that isn't enough he then pulls out of the Republican Party and starts his own Party and lo and behold he runs away with the popular vote, and almost gets enough electoral votes to win it all. And here I am, a political reporter and I don't have a clue who is really behind Mark Worthington – you know the operatives, the money people, the politicians who make things happen! So, don't you think a story about these unknown string pullers would make an interesting story? Who are they? Where did they come from? How did they manage to all come together at one time? You know, how did they manage to create the 'perfect storm' that has resulted in this non-politician attracting so many votes, and getting to the point where he may yet get enough electoral votes to win it all."

"Yes, Mr.Christopher- Theodore White, Junior, I do think it would make one helluva story!"

"And really now, wouldn't you like to know what is going on with the Democrats and the Republican losers right now? How are they taking their dethroning at the hands of this upstart? Are they going to take it gracefully and just roll over? Or are they going to raise all kinds of hell to try and keep him from taking office. I just think it has all the makings of a great story!"

Cyndy didn't respond right away but just studied her husband for a minute or so. She thought 'he really does get excited about things once in a while, but she hadn't seen him this excited in a very long time.

Finally, she answered his question "I think you've hit on a great idea and obviously you're really excited about it. When you think about it this election isn't about the 'making of a President' but really it's about 'the making of a third party strong enough to elect a president'. *That* is pretty heady stuff – really heady stuff! But before you do anything why don't you Google it and find out if anybody actually has written about what happened?"

Chris got up from his seat and walked around the table to where Cyndy was sitting and he leaned over and put his arms around her and gave her a big kiss, saying "I love the way you understand me and support everything I want to do, and your Google idea is a good one."

Cyndy pulled back and looked up at him and said "Whoa there, Kimmasavee, who said anything about either understanding you or supporting all of your crazy ideas? I said I liked this one a lot – so don't go getting any early morning romantic ideas. I suggest you march yourself into your study and jot down some of these ideas , do a Google search while I see if I can find Cissy Gonzalez – 'cause I think you are going to need a lot of help from her – a lot!"

Chapter 6

Gov. Bobby Houston had barely closed his eyes all night long, and between being glued to at least four television sets, and conferring with his top political hands every thirty minutes, he had one major all-consuming headache. His eyes were so tired they just ached. But he was bound and determined to sit here in his command center until hell freezes over if there is any chance he can do something to prevent Mark Worthington from winning the Presidency outright.

He shouted across the room to his Communications chief "Get me the mayors of El Paso, San Antonio, Dallas, Plano and Houston on the phone. I'll take them one at a time, and I will let them know how damn close they are to being ruined politically if they don't figure out some way to make those ballots come out favoring me!"

The mayor of El Paso was the first one his staff was able to reach, and the Governor sat down and put his feet up on his desk and picking up the phone, he snarled "Rodrique, how do you like being a big time mayor in Texas?"

Rodrique was stunned by the sheer malevolence in Houston's voice as he responded "Good morning Governor. Uh, I like being mayor of El Paso a lot. I think we are doing some really good things out here, and making progress on a lot of different fronts. Why do you ask?"

In a voice that was so low, the mayor could hardly hear him, Bobby Houston said "Because you slimy wetback, if you don't get hold of those absentee ballots and make absolutely, totally sure that they are all counted for me, then your political career is over, and you might just as well sign up to pick cotton next spring, because you sure as hell aren't going to be drawing down the big time salary you are earning right now. Do I make myself perfectly clear?"

"Yes sir. But.."

Bobby Houston exploded into the phone "No buts, you worthless piece of shit! Just do what I told you to do!" With that he slammed the phone down, and yelled to his aide:

"Put the next ass-hole on!"

The governor then proceeded to repeat the conversation he had just completed with Rodrique only now with the mayors of Houston, Dallas, Plano and San Antonio. He slammed the phone down one last time, and turning to his chief of staff he said, "I think they got the message. I don't give a Texas rat's ass if they like what I told them to do. If they want to have any future in this state, in this political party, they damn well better get to those ballots and get my name punched in or get rid of any that favor Worthington. It's just as easy as that!"

"Aren't you afraid there might be some backlash?" his chief of staff ventured.

"No, I'm not afraid of any 'backlash' as you call it. They don't dare cross me or their careers are toast. So let's see just how clever they are."

■■■

The Mayor of El Paso, Rodrique Castillo, was a sixth generation Hispanic-American. He had been educated at Texas

A&M and married to an anglo that he had met at the University of Texas Law School.

 As he hung up the phone, he turned to his Administrative aide, and said "Cancel any appointments or appearances on my schedule for today and tomorrow. I'm going home and unless there is a clear 4-alarm emergency please don't try to reach me. I'll probably see you on Friday."

Rodrique's driver was waiting and as he got into the car, he said "Phil, just take me home. I have a lot of thinking to do, and I can't get it done here." With that the driver left the parking lot and headed toward the Mayor's residence.

■ ■

The car pulled into the driveway, and Rodrique thanked his driver and very briskly left the car and moved up the driveway into the house. His wife Cynthia was on the phone when he came into the foyer. She gave a quick wave to him and then quickly ended the call coming out to meet him.

"I thought you were booked up all day today. What's up with you coming home at 9:30? I'm sure glad I didn't have a boy friend in here!"

"Very funny. I have a big time personal crisis on my hands and I need to talk to you about it."

"Rod, what the hell is going on? I haven't seen you like this in – well honestly I don't think I have *ever* seen you like this. What happened?"

He quickly repeated the call from Bobby Houston, and then added "I have not told anyone about the call, although I did record it."

"Good for you. So what do you think you're going to do?"

"Well, first of all, think about what I am being asked to do. I am being asked to somehow intercept thousands of absentee ballots and in some way make them look like they are for Houston, or at least not for Mark Worthington."

"But, he's lost the election. Why in the world would he want you to do that?"

He then briefly explained the electoral college stalemate and how the results in Texas could possibly keep Worthington from winning the election outright, thus throwing it into the House of Representatives.

"The Republicans have a majority in the House right now, and probably will still have the largest number of votes in the next session, so Houston figures that he would have a better than average chance of getting elected – *if* the election goes into the House

She continued, "So he wants you to 'steal' the ballots and mess with them somehow so that he can win the election? Is he serious?"

"Cynthia, he is totally serious. But what I didn't tell you is that in the middle of this little hissy-fit, he actually called me a 'wetback', and he threatened to ruin my political career if I didn't do what he wants."

"You? A wetback? Oh, my God! What unmitigated gall. Who in the hell does he think is?"

"Honestly, I don't know who he thinks he is, but he sounded like a mad man on the phone: mean, surly, cruel, just about everything bad you could imagine. It was scary, really scary!"

"Alright, so what *are* your options Rod? You have always been really good about laying out options."

"Well, I guess I could just get a couple of my close friends to hi-jack the absentee ballot truck, or break into the counting room and mess up all the ballots……."

Cynthia looked at him with a look that was a cross between total amazement and total scorn. "If anyone found out what you did, you would go to prison, you know that don't you?"

"Exactly! In which case my political career would be ruined anyhow. Right?"

"Right. So forget that stupid idea. What's the next option?"

The next option would be to simply ignore him and pretend that I *tried* to do something but couldn't make it happen. You know stuff like security was too tight. Too many poll watchers. Too many cops. All the reasons why I couldn't get to the ballots. And by the way, those *are* all good reasons. Then I would just put my head down, apologize and hope he forgets what he said he would do to me."

"You know honey, that just does not sound like you. Put your head down and apologize? I don't think so! Tell me what you really are thinking about."

He smiled knowing that she would see through all those dopey ideas, then said "Okay. Here is what I think I *am* going to do. First of all, I am going to make absolutely, positively certain that all of those absentee ballots are counted just as they were filled out. I am going to call in extra city police and tell everyone that I had an anonymous call that someone might be trying to break into the counting room and tamper with the ballots. I'm going to do the exact opposite of what he asked me to do!"

"Sounds good so far."

"Starting today I am going to call the mayors in all of the 10 largest cities in Texas and see if any of them had a similar call. I may end up having to tell some of them that I taped the call and that I am notifying the Federal attorney for this area, and that I am going public with the information on Monday. I am also going to resign as Mayor this afternoon, and I am going to encourage all of the other mayors he may have contacted to do the same thing. *That* is what I am going to do!"

"Wow! Now that sounds more like the man I sleep with!" With that she got up and went around to where he was sitting and put her arms around him and gave him one great big, delicious full mouth kiss."

"It's going to be rough for a while Cyn. It is probably going to be very rough. But I cannot sit still and let this man – I might call him this madman - get away with something like this. Of course, I don't want to go to jail, but my God, that isn't even a consideration. I don't want anything to do with some kind of conspiracy to fix an election? For God's sake that undermines the very basic foundation of our democracy – our right to a secret ballot!"

Cyndy thought for a moment and then she said "Houston could go to jail for even attempting to do this. I'm sure he could at least be indicted."

"Maybe. But once it is out in the open he'll be ruined as far as any future in politics is concerned. So even if I ruin my own political future, I will at least have eliminated Dr. Strangelove from the political scene.

"Another thing. I'm going underground for a few days, so get the kids ready to get out of town tonight. I know a place where we can all go and no one will be able to find us. It'll be fun to have a couple of days together, but I don't want any interviews or calls, or interference. Can you be ready to leave tonight?"

She looked up at him and with a smile on her face said, "I bet I know exactly where you are taking us, so you bet. We'll be ready when you are!"

Rod, stood up and leaned over and gave her a quick kiss on the forehead and said, "Thanks, my love. I knew you would understand. But, now I have some phone calls to make. Thanks for hearing me out."

****

Mayor Castillo made a list of ten of the largest and most prominent mayors in the state that he planned on calling. His first calls were to the mayors of Lubbock, Midland, Plano, and Waco asking them if anyone had called asking them to tamper with absentee ballots. They all said no and none of them except the Mayor of Plano seemed the least bit ill at ease with him on the phone. So, he didn't go into any of the details with them. Then finally he placed a call to the Mayor of San Antonio. The response was just short of being surreal.

"Just who do you think might have contacted me with such a scheme?" was the initial response. Rod knew that he had struck pay dirt.

He said, "Bill, you don't need to beat around the bush with me. If you received a call, and I think you did, you know damn well who it was from, so what I am asking you is 'what are you going to do about it'?"

The response continued to be a bit vague. "Well, if I did get such a call, and I am not saying that I did, what business is it of yours what I do about it?"

Rod answered, "Okay, I'm through being coy with you about this thing. Here is what *I'm* going to do. I am going public on Monday and along with the Federal Attorney at my side, I am going to tell the world what the Governor of this state asked me to do *for* him, and *to* the people of Texas. I am also resigning as Mayor on Friday, so that there won't be any doubt in anyone's mind as to my sincerity. He is asking me to commit a crime, and I suspect he has asked you to commit a similar crime. So here is the bottom line: I'm asking you to think it over, and give me a call on Friday. I'd be absolutely thrilled if you joined me at the microphones when we drop this on our erstwhile Governor."

The Mayor of San Antonio paused for a very long time and then in a very quiet voice said, "I taped my phone call as well, Rod. I just haven't decided what to do. I promise you that I will call you early Friday with my decision. Thanks for the call. And by the way: good luck!"

He could not get through to either the Dallas or Houston mayors, but he left a rather urgent message asking them to get in touch with him as soon as possible.

Okay, he thought. "Tomorrow I call the Federal attorney, and get this thing off the ground."

Chapter 7

The Reverend Jimmy Foxworthy had been the leading Republican candidate for President as recently as a month before the primary season began. But then a long list of candidates including Senator Ellen Livingston, the only serious female in the race, entered the contest. Finally Texas Governor Bobby Houston jumped in and managed to take away a great deal of the very conservative, religious right support which Foxworthy thought he owned.

Thing weren't going as smoothly as Jimmy had hoped during the primary, but he was piling up a fairly substantial number of delegate votes, when suddenly during the nominating convention he had abruptly abandoned the race announcing his support for Bobby Houston, who in turn quickly chose him to be his Vice Presidential running mate. There had never been any good explanation coming from either Foxworthy himself, or from the Bobby Houston camp concerning just what went on, but obviously there had been a deal made to make Foxworthy the Vice Presidential candidate to get him to give up his own campaign. But, the why was never explained and neither party made any effort to clear up the mystery.

Now Foxworthy was waiting to hear from Gov. Houston to get his marching orders. Because neither candidate got enough electoral votes to win outright, it certainly looked like there was a strong possibility that the race was headed to the House of Representatives.

Foxworthy had been a loyal campaigner but had been relegated to back water cities by the candidate. They had only gotten together twice during the entire campaign, and among his immediate staff he made no bones for his dislike of Bobby Drew Houston.

He turned to Jay McCauliff his campaign manager and said "Wouldn't you know that red-neck son of a bitch would pull a trick like that – trying to fix the ballots so that he could be sure to win the Texas electoral votes. What was he thinking? Those votes weren't enough to get him over the top. Now look at him. Ruined! He won't win an election for dog catcher in McAllen, Texas after this mess!"

Jay responded "Maybe on second thought we shouldn't have dropped out of the race when we did?"

"Look, Jay, we had no choice – ya hear me? We had no choice. He got something on me – complete with pictures – and I don't want to go into it. Okay? But, I'll tell you what. I'm not gonna shed any tears over that bastard's fall. He deserves to fall, and I hope he suffers from it – a lot!"

Jay turned away and quickly changed the subject. Obviously his boss didn't want to talk about that subject, but he couldn't help but wonder – "had something on him – including pictures! He thought to himself ….Right after he met with Houston was when he sent that bimbo packing, and he hasn't been happy since. Not the same guy. No fire in his belly. We tried to warn him that she was trouble, but he wouldn't listen. Damn! His poor wife knew he was banging that trailer trash every night, but she couldn't stand up to him. She's a poor little mouse. And behind all that holier than thou shit, he is little more than just a big prick! So why am I sticking around here? Surely there's some one out there I can hook up with who isn't a slime bag like these two. God, I've got to get out of here!"

****

Three days later Jay McCauliffe submitted his resignation to Jimmy Foxworthy, wishing him well in his future political life. He had to bite his tongue as he wrote this, because he didn't think this Okie had any future whatsoever, but why rub it in.

He also called Foxworthy's wife and told her of his decision and wished her well also. Her response to him was totally unexpected.

"Jay, thank you so much for thinking of me before you left. It's pretty obvious that no one else in that group around Jimmy has ever given me a second thought. But I want you to know that I am done with this part of my life. My lawyer is filing for divorce from Jimmy tomorrow. He wants to bed that tramp singer so he can have her. I'm hoping that my leaving him will really screw up his future political life. I have been so humiliated by his screwing around all these years, that I just can't take it one more day. Tomorrow, he has to find some place else to live, and my guess is that Mr. Wanna be President may end up sleeping in a double wide with his white trash. Isn't that the ultimate? Anyhow, thanks again Jay. I appreciate your consideration."

Jay could barely come up with a response to her, other than to say, "I'm so sorry. So very sorry. I hated all those trips we made where you stayed behind, and he was all over that tramp. But what could I say? He acted as if no one had any idea what was going on, and you know, boys will be boys. I, I just hated it! But short of resigning in the middle of the campaign what could I do? I'm just so sorry that all of this has come down to this. What a damn shame.

"Please let me know if there is anything I can do to help you, and I mean anything. If you need any depositions or anything, just let me know. I'll be happy to see him go down in flames!"

****

After Jay hung up the phone he sat for a few minutes and considered the runaway train wreck this whole campaign had been, and how close Bobby Houston and Jimmy Foxworthy had come to becoming the President and Vice President of the United States. It just brought a chill over him.

But then the thought occurred to him: "the Electors from Arkansas are not legally committed to vote for the candidate who carried the election, so maybe, just maybe he could prevail on them to vote their conscience, and vote for Mark Worthington. That would push Worthington even closer to an outright win, and avoid all the ugliness of the House of

Chapter 8

Bryce Randolph walked out the front door of his Sun City West house and down the drive way to pick up the Arizona Republic and the Wall Street Journal as he did almost every day at home, and he marveled to himself just how clear the sky was and how promising the weather forecast for the day had been. But then the weather forecast in Arizona was the same almost every day. Every day was almost like every other day: clear, warm, dry and beautiful. And this time of year was what most everyone was looking forward to after a long, warm or should we say hot summer. So now it was just one nice day after another! "Long live boring!"

Bryce Randolph had been retired for a few years when he decided to write an unsolicited letter to Senator Jeff Cochran in a moment of frustration. He just wanted to know what the Senator thought about some of the major political and social issues of the day. There was no way he could have imagined, in his wildest dreams, of the fall out from that letter. He had become swept up in a movement to organize political discussion groups among Senior Citizens that ended up with him being appointed the Director of the entire national movement. He spent way more than half of his time organizing groups of these seniors in all fifty states, and collating their findings – first for the Republican Party and later for Mark Worthington's fledgling group.

He never much thought of himself as a politician, but by the time the primaries passed by and the election itself was held on Tuesday, he realized that he had not only crossed the threshold into the political arena, but that he had really enjoyed the journey. But now he was finally home, and except for a few mandatory appearances coming up in the not too distant future, he could, at last, slip back into his pre-election self and enjoy reading, spending time with his wife, and playing some golf with the many friends he had made over the years.

Bryce took in a great big breath of fresh air and was about to return to the house when Bill Farmer, his golfing buddy of many years drove up in his golf cart.

"Bryce, it's really good to see you! It's been a long time what with all of your work getting the new President elected. Are you going to start playing again? Or like Roger likes to say, are you going to be Secretary of State or some damn thing like that?"

Bryce just laughed as he put his foot on the cart and both hands on the top twisting his fingers in the outlandish fringe that they had installed around the top. "No, Bill, I am going to start playing golf in a couple of weeks, and I am not going to become Secretary of State or anything else. Believe me I've about had it with politics for awhile. But, as far as my man Mark becoming President, I'm really happy that he is as close as he is, but I guess we won't know for sure for a couple of more days. But I sure hope that he gets those last few electoral votes."

Bill asked "You got to know him pretty well during the campaign didn't you?'

"Oh, yeah, I sure did, and Bill I'll tell you what. He is one helluva guy! He's the real thing! I just hope that he gets over the hump this week – and then maybe Jaclyn and I can wrangle an invite to the inauguration."

Bill Farmer started to laugh as he said "Oh, boy, and to think I knew you when – now just when was it? Back in the good old days when you couldn't make a four foot putt if your life depended on it! And now here you are - about to go off dancin' at the Presidential ball. Can I touch you old buddy?" He reached over with a finger pointing toward Bryce's sleeve.

Bryce was laughing out loud by this time, and he finished their conversation with "Why don't you just kiss my ring first, before you are welcome to kiss something else my old friend! But it's really good to see you. I missed you guys!"

Bill said, "Sure you missed us. Like a toothache you missed us. Traveling all around the country; meeting all those important people; eating $100 dollar meals; drinking $100 dollar bottles of wine; getting to know a famous General and now probably our next President! Sure you missed us!"

"No, no, no! Really, I am so glad to be home and in my own bed, I can't begin to tell you how good it feels. I just need a few days to get my head screwed on right. But I promise, I will call you in a week or so when I've finally put my life back in order - and we can start playing some golf again. And by the way, it was you, Mr.Yips, who couldn't make the four foot putts, remember? It wasn't me!"

Bryce stepped back, and Bill pulled away with a final "We'll all look forward to getting you back on the course, and getting some of your money – which is long overdue. Actually, that is what I missed!"

****

Bryce went into the house where Jaclyn was in the process of making a couple of eggs over medium. She had put some sour dough toast in the toaster and that was really smelling good. She said "Where did you have to go to get the papers? You sure were gone long enough."

"Oh, Bill Farmer pulled up in his golf cart just as I went to pick them up and we chatted for a few minutes. He wanted to know if I'm going to be the next Secretary of State."

"Oh, sure, I can see it now. 'President submits name of a seventy-something retired consultant from nowhere in Arizona, with no prior experience, and mono-lingual at that, to be our next Secretary of State.' Now, I'd guess that Letterman might have some fun with that one, like the Top Ten reasons why that wouldn't be a good idea!"

"Yeah, I guess that really is pretty funny when you think about it. But anyhow Bill wants to know when I can start playing golf again – says he wants some of my money."

"You guys! What do you play for? Is it $1.00 per guy at best? He could win every time you play and at the end of the year he'd probably have enough to buy an upper deck ticket to a Suns game."

Bryce turned to her and said, "Well, I'm not *that* incompetent. Maybe I could be Secretary of the Treasury since I've been so successful in letting dollar bills slip through my hands! With that he turned on the television and asked "What's new with the election? Any more results in?"

"No, as far as I can see, it is still the same as when we went to bed last night. Mark is almost there, but not quite. He and Janet just have to be dying. And poor Gordon! He's too old to have this much stress to live with!"

"What's this talking head saying?" as he leaned closer to the TV. "They think there may be some monkey business with the counting of the absentee ballots in Illinois and Texas. Crap! Don't tell me that a bunch of sleazy politicians in Chicago are going to try and stuff the ballot boxes so that the President can take Illinois away from Mark.

"For God's sake we don't do things like that anymore, or do we? Old Dick Daley is long dead and his son has also retired, so who is going to pull off something like that today?"

"Well, isn't the Mayor a former big dealie in the White House?"

Bryce thought for a minute and quietly replied "Yeah, I suppose he might be able to orchestrate something like that, but I think it might even be hard for him to do."

"Well, dear, don't you go getting your blood pressure all exercised over it. There is nothing – not one damn thing – that you can do about the situation, so just relax. You want me to switch from the news to the Golf Channel?"

"No, no, no! You are absolutely right of course. But it just makes me sick to my stomach that we still have a political system where there is even a possibility that an election in this country could be rigged. It's like 'hello, Virginia, and welcome to the eighteenth century!' It's really just sad, Jaclyn, just plain sad!"

Jaclyn got the last word in with "At least nothing has happened yet, so maybe nothing will."

Chapter 9

The mayor of Chicago sat in his office after he hung up talking to Wally Backstrom and he turned to the two people sitting in his office. Sandy Jasperson was his very able chief of staff, and Martin Jackson was his number one political aide. Sandy's main job was to keep track of the patronage issues because the people who owed their jobs to the mayor would also be expected to support him politically. Jackson was the power behind delivering the enormous black vote in the city. The two of them together made a very potent support team for the mayor who was still getting his feet wet after succeeding the last of the Daleys.

Sandy spoke first. "Did you have the recorder going on that call?"

"I did. So what do you think?"

Sandy replied, "I think he's gone off his rocker! That's what I think."

Marty then added "Does he really think we can just dig up 100,000 or so cemetery votes, just like that? If I hadn't heard it with my own ears I would have said you must be kidding me. Man, that's some pretty big trash talk."

"Okay, okay, so it was a lot of pretty strong trash talk, but let's get real serious for a minute. Can he hurt me, personally or politically?"

Sandy said, "I think if by some miracle he should manage to arrange things so that they get thrown into the House, and by an equally large miracle, he should carry the day and get re-elected, if all those things happen, then he probably can hurt you some. He can deny patronage, he can arrange that your pet projects get overlooked, he can even come in and campaign against you in the next election. So, sure, he could hurt you. But remember, there will have to be two miracles first!"

Marty then added "Hasn't anyone told him just how unpopular he is? He isn't a Bill Clinton, and he sure as hell isn't a Barack and he isn't close to being an LBJ! He finished dead last among the three candidates – imagine that! A sitting President runs *third* in a Presidential election! That has got to tell you something.

"Anyhow, for what it's worth, I go to Church every Sunday because, believe it or not, I do have some beliefs, but primarily because it is politically a smart thing to do, and I have never put a lot of stock in miracles. And miracles like you're talking about sure as hell ain't going to happen right here in good old Chicago on the shores of Lake Michigan."

"I hear you. You know perfectly well that I have no use for the guy – the way he treated all of the staff after the death of the President. You would have thought he could have been a little more considerate, but no, out the door they went – rude note to follow! But I think we have to consider what our response should be and then just how we communicate it. Here's what I'm thinking. Let's send a bunch of our most trusted people to the various places where they are counting votes, but give them no specific instructions accept that we sure want to carry the state for the President – nothing more than that. Then we get back to Washington and tell them that we sent a whole lot of good solid Democrats out and they just couldn't manage to change the results very much.

"But, I'll tell you what. We have that conversation on tape. I want a statement from each of you, signed by you, that you heard the conversation and that you didn't hear me agree to anything. I hate to put you two guys in this position, but if I have to blow the whistle on the President I want some support *guaranteed!*"

Sandy asked "Do you think he asked Backstrom to call anyone else?"

Marty answered "That's a really good question. But I think we might have heard if he did make other calls. Who's he gonna call? There are way too many Republicans out there for him to have much luck with Governors, or with mayors, for that matter. No, I think he thinks the 'Daley machine lives on and that they can fix anything!"

The mayor sat back in a typical judge pose, with his fingers peaked together. "He also has to know that I really don't much care whether he gets elected or not. The way he cut all those people that were close to our old boss- not to mention me. Does he think we just sit out here turning our cheek? He put a lot of good people out of work, and just cut the guts out of a really good political team. Now there isn't anyone in the big house who can stand up to him and tell him what is really going on. So he just goes on his merry way thinking that the American public really loves him, and that he can order anyone in the Party to commit a crime to try and fix this election which he can't win by himself. God almighty, that really is sick!"

Sandy stood up and said "I'm going to get those people out to the various places where the ballots are being counted, so just let me know when you have that statement ready. I'll be happy to sign it!"

Marty nodded in agreement as he too rose and moved to the door.

****

A few minutes later the Mayor's secretary stuck her head into his office and said, "Mr. Mayor, Jeremiah Brady is on the phone. Says it is urgent that he talk to you. Do you want me to plug him into you?"

The Mayor looked up with a puzzled look and said, "Sure, I'll talk to Jerry."

"Hello, Jerry! How are things with you. The election sure didn't turn out the way the President hoped, but that's the way politics goes, I guess."

"Things are not so good with me or the President." Brady then proceeded to fill the Mayor in on what happened that morning in the Oval Office.

"So, he really did tell Backstrom to call me. What the hell was he thinking? We can't go around forging names and stuffing ballot boxes. That kind of stuff died with the first Daley – not even the kid could pull off any of that stuff anymore. But, go on. What happened to you?"

Brady then described the scene where he tried to straight talk the President about his lack of popularity and just why he ran such a poor third in the election. "He just exploded! I honestly was getting ready to take a punch – he was that angry with what I said!"

"Well, he's been under a lot of pressure, and I'm sure he didn't think for a New York minute that he was going to run third out of three!"

"No, I'm sure he didn't, but he was like a mad man, totally out of control and totally unwilling to listen to reality! He actually thinks that the American public loves him and that some great conspiracy has denied him the election! I'm not kidding you, bizarre is the only way you can describe it."

"So he fired you?"

"On the spot. Told me to clear out my desk and take my team with me. He even suggested that we had been working behind his back in some way to be sure that he lost the election! It was just bizarre, that's what it was! But, anyhow, can I be so bold as to ask you what you are going to do?"

"I'm not going to do a damn thing except to send up a smoke-screen meant to confuse a lot of people, but not change one single vote. *That* is what I'm going to do. And, oh, yes, I'm also going to find a job for you my friend. I need people like you around here.

Chapter 10

Senator Jeff Corcoran left Mark Worthington's hotel room and made his way down a couple of floors to his own suite where Nancy was sitting with the morning newspaper while periodically glancing over at the television set in the corner.

As Jeff let himself into the room, Nancy looked up and said, "Hey there, 'O thou great and worthy master!" This was a favorite greeting that Jeff had made her say in the first days of their marriage and she continued it all these years.

"How did things go up there this morning?"

Jeff laughed as he acknowledged the greeting, and then on a more somber note he replied, "Well, everyone was disappointed, of course, that Mark hadn't won it all outright – at least as of this morning. But it was a pretty serious discussion. Cody summarized where we are and the importance of Mark winning one of those two big states, Illinois or Texas.

Nancy got up to pour more coffee for both of them. "How do you feel about the chances that he can carry one of them?

"Not real good. He's ahead by a hair in Texas and behind a little in Illinois. And even if he wins Maryland he won't have enough electoral votes."

Nancy slapped her hand down on the table and said, "Damn this Electoral vote thing! I never did understand that whole thing, and now it may keep Mark from getting elected? That is just a crying shame!"

"Well, it is what it is, and at this point we can't do anything about it. Maybe, we can set up a Senate committee to look into how we could change the system to prevent this happening again, but for now we just have to sit and sweat it out!'

Nancy grumbled under her breathe and said "Sure, I know I should be patient, but it just ticks me off ….. so read me my rights, and I'll go away!"

Jeff laughed, and looking over at her he said, "Alright Mrs. Corcoran, you have the right to remain silent……"

With that Nancy had to laugh as well.

"At least we are still sane enough to laugh a little. Mark wants to have one more meeting this afternoon, just to see if anything new has popped up; then we can un-circle the wagons and get back to our offices and homes. I was thinking that maybe we could catch a flight tonight to Ohio and spend a couple of days there before we head back to Washington. Whaddya think about that?"

"You know what? Unless you have some urgent business to take care of in Ohio – do you?"

Jeff nodded negatively, and Nancy then continued "In that case why don't we just drive to our home in Arlington. It would really be nice to be at home over the weekend and just kind of catch our breath. You know what I mean?"

"Yeah, I do know what you mean and I think you are absolutely right. No matter what happens over the next few days being here – or in Ohio isn't going to help us any. We'll be far better off being in Washington – home, kids, my office, my staff!

God, I am glad that I thought of that – sure hope you agree?" he laughed as Nancy just shook her head, smiling all the while.

"Sometimes Mr.C you just have these wonderful ideas and I am *SO* lucky to be near you to validate them. It's just wonderful how those things work out! I'll call and make sure they know we'll be home tonight. Do you think we can get out of here by 8 or 9 tonight?"

"I can't imagine our meeting going very late, but you know what? Let's stay here tonight, get a good night's sleep and then leave first thing in the morning. I think I like that even better."

Nancy looked at him and said "This time I do like your idea – and for a change it really was your idea! Tomorrow it is!"

Chapter 11

The morning after a national Presidential election is tough on a lot of people. Reporters are up for nearly 24 hours and after awhile the numbers begin to blur and the results become fuzzy. The candidates who had the temerity to challenge an incumbent and lost are disappointed beyond words. The challengers who win however are generally overcome with a combination of feelings. They are euphoric simply by virtue of having won; they are overwhelmed as they think of the job ahead and as they begin to comprehend the really hard work and assumption of responsibility that lies just a day or two ahead.

Incumbents who are defeated are hugely disappointed and tend to begin seeing shadows of conspiracy everywhere related to how any upstart could have ejected them from the public trough. However, incumbents who have won generally feel grateful that their constituents have seen fit to return them for another few years, and relieved that they don't have to upend their families and staff like the defeated candidates have to do.

Then there are the candidates who were fortunate enough to have a position like two-thirds of those in the United States Senate who don't have to run in a Presidential election year. However smug they may be they too are tired on the Wednesday after the election because they have always stayed up late watching the results and pulling for those candidates of their own party who they may have campaigned for. And of course they have more than a passing interest in both the Presidential race, and all of the Congressional races. After all it is the President they will have to support, or perhaps fight with that will be an immense factor in determining how successful they are. Then, too, the people who will be sitting with them on the floor of the Congress will also play a very important part in their lives for at least the next two years.

So, it was not at all unusual for Senator Ellen Livingston, Republican from New Jersey, to be a bit groggy when she rolled out of bed around 8:30am on the day after the election. After splashing some water on her face, she moved into the sitting room of the Hotel in Trenton where she had joined hundreds of other Republican supporters as they watched the results of both the national election and all of the state wide contests as well.

Ellen was long considered to be one of the most eligible single people in Washington. She had gone through a divorce many years before, and after a couple of years she had decided to start dating, although on a very infrequent and casual basis. She had a friend, an ex-NFL quarterback whom she saw two or three times a year, and with whom she enjoyed a very satisfactory sex life. But there was no love there and with her work in the Senate and his work on the West Coast there was almost no chance that anything serious would develop.

After she made herself a cup of coffee she clicked on the television to see what had happened after she finally crashed around 2am.She joined a long list of others who were shocked to find out that the Presidential election was still up in the air. She immediately reached for the phone and placed a call to her closest friend in Washington and frequent dinner partner, Senator Bob Madison. She called his personal cell and he immediately picked up.

"Hello, my favorite Republican! So what do *you* think about the news this morning?"

Ellen laughed and said "Well at least the feeling is mutual, because you are definitely my favorite Democrat! What do I think? Well, I thought Mark had it put away last night, and I'm really surprised that it is still up for grabs. God, I hope that it doesn't go into the House!"

Bob was a very moderate Democrat from Wisconsin and was part of the group of twelve bi-partisan and dissident Senators who often met during the years to discuss key issues. Made up of six Republicans and six Democrats they unanimously supported Ellen's decision to put her name into the hat for the Republican nomination for President. They all felt that she would make one helluva President and the fact that she just happened to be a woman made her just that much more formidable. Unfortunately for Ellen the far right dominated the Primaries and the Convention and Ellen was effectively shut out. When Mark Worthington was also rejected by the Convention, she was a proud supporter of his effort to win the Presidency as an Independent.

Bob said, "I'd have to agree with you there. But I think there is still a good chance that Mark will carry either Texas or Illinois."

She replied "I sure hope you are right. He would be so right for the job, and neither of those other guys can hold a candle to him."

"Well, it seems to me, on a personal basis, Mark Worthington as President would put you squarely in the Political spotlight. I know it is none of my business, but has he offered you any kind of position in his administration, should he finally win the thing?"

"All he said to me was he really looked forward to working with me if he won – no specifics – no offers. But you know what Bob? I don't really want a job in the Administration. I want to help him get support from the Senate, and I think that is going to be very dicey with three political parties vying for control."

"Well, I can certainly see you as the Leader of the third party, small as it is right now. But, I will tell you something – I don't think that I am the only Senator who is currently reassessing his party affiliation. I think that small group of ten or twelve currently committed to the Independence Party could grow substantially over the next couple of months!"

"That's interesting! I have felt that we might pick up three or four more seats, but I'm not sure what would trigger any more than that to move into our area.

"But speaking of 'our areas' it sounds like you are going to seat yourself with the Democrats – at least to start with?'

"Yeah, I think that makes sense for me right now, but as I said, depending on what finally happens with the Presidency I might just change my mind and move into your area. Anyhow, I much prefer your company than any of the liberal jerks in my party! Besides, I'd like to sit closer to you!"

Ellen was laughing when she responded "Well speaking of getting seated and stuff like that, when are you coming back to Washington?"

"I'm leaving tomorrow. The current leader has called for a caucus Thursday afternoon so I need to be there for that."

"Have any plans for this weekend?"

"Ah, that sounds like a leading question. What do you have in mind?"

"Well, I just happened to book a small house on the Jersey shore for the weekend. I'll be driving down early Friday evening and I'd love to have you join me – that is if you can tear yourself away from all of those beautiful Washington ladies I read about all the time!"

Bob Madison had been a favorite dinner companion of Ellen's for a long time and there had never been much time for anything real serious but over the last few months they had gotten much closer. He often thought that if he was to get married again, Ellen would be his absolute number one choice. "Even if I had an appointment to fly to the moon, I would cancel the plans to be able to join you at the shore."

"Since I know where the place is, how about my picking you up at your place about 7?"

"Perfect. I can't wait to see you!"

Chapter 12

Governor Earl Potts had returned home after voting on Tuesday and immediately put in calls to Ernie Hardesty and Charlie Wipperman and invited them to join him for breakfast the day after the election – to review what had happened on election day and get caught up on all of their personal lives which had been put pretty much on hold during the campaign.

Charlie Wipperman was a very successful John Deere farm equipment retailer out of Clear Lake, Iowa and he had deep ties to the Republican Party, former Senator and now Senator elect Ernie Hardesty and Governor Earl Potts. He got up early the morning after the election even though he had stayed up until nearly midnight watching the results with his wife and a few friends. He decided to leave the house early and stop at the McDonalds just south of town for a quick egg-McMuffin breakfast and a large coffee.

It had appeared almost 100% certain when he finally went to bed the night before that Iowa had cast not only a majority of its votes for Mark Worthington but they had done so in resounding fashion. With all but a handful of absentee ballots counted Iowa had voted 57% for Mark, 28% for Bobby Houston and only 15% for the President. He was still shaking his head over that result. What an unbelievable difference four years had made – it just didn't seem possible! But there it was. But he also thought to himself, "What happens now? What happens to the old parties? What happens to the new Party on the block? Five of the seven representatives from the state are now members of the new party, as is Ernie Hardesty. But Earl Potts is still the sitting Governor – as a Republican!

As he got into his car to leave McDonalds, he found himself talking to himself, but out loud "How are we going to make any sense out of all of this. I sure hope that is what Earl wants to talk about. Wonder if Ernie will be there?"

****

Ernie Hardesty, fresh off his election victory, and return to the U.S. Senate was in the Governor's office when Charlie walked in. There were congratulations and warm feelings expressed all around concerning the election results.

Then the Governor turned serious and said, "You know guys, this election has really turned a lot of things upside down. Here you are Ernie, a Senator-elect having won on the Independence Party ticket. Charlie you've already resigned from the Republican Party and taken control of the Independence Party in the State, and I'm still the Republican Governor! What's wrong with this picture?"as he put his arms out with the palms up in a 'what's going on' sort of plea.

Charlie Wipperman spoke up "Well, the facts are exactly as you described them Earl. The Republican Party in the state is in a shambles, and the Democrats – well you can hardly describe the mess they are in. Everyone knows that you came out and endorsed Mark Worthington for President, so I guess the next move is up to you."

Ernie Hardesty joined in with "Earl, I think Charlie is right. It looks to me like if you stay in the Republican party you are going to be looked at as some sort of a pariah. You deserted the

Party's candidate when you came out for Mark, and you made no bones about what you thought of Bobby Houston! Honestly, I don't see that you have much choice."

The two old friends looked closely as Earl seemed to be struggling with his thoughts. Then finally he said, "There were a lot of Independents elected to the legislature this time, so I think I'll have quite a lot of support, so I think I'm going to announce tomorrow, that I am resigning from the Republican Party and registering as a member of the Independence Party. Hell, I only have a little over a year left until the next Governor's race. I can get through that long a period with one hand tied behind my back!"

"Good man, Earl, Good man!" Ernie said as he shook Earl's hand for an extended period of time.

"Hell, we're going to have an Independence Party President for at least four years, so what's the worst that can happen? Looks to me like the worst is if one of the other two parties really gets its act together and somehow makes us irrelevant. So the real question is this: has our American political system now changed for good, with three parties sharing power? Or is this a temporary thing, that's likely to dissolve just as quickly as it appeared? That's your big question!"

Charlie and Earl sat very silently absorbing what Ernie has just said, and they both knew in their hearts that this was in fact the reality of the situation, and that no one, no one, had any clear idea what lay ahead for all of them.

Chapter 13

It was very early on Thursday after the election and the President was sitting at his desk when his Secretary buzzed him. "The Attorney General is on the line, and he says it is very important. Do you want to speak with him?"

"Sure, put him on. He can't bring me any more bad news than I have already had this week."

The President picked up the phone and very brusquely said "What's up?"

The answer nearly knocked him off his chair. "There may have been some ballot irregularities in Texas and I need to come over and brief you."

"Why don't you just tell me what you learned?"

"I would rather not. I need to meet with you one on one. Give me a time."

A sitting President isn't used to subordinates demanding meeting time, but the AG sounded really serious, so he decided to agree to his rather impertinent request, and not just tell him to go 'piss off'.

"Okay, I'm pretty busy today, how about 4 o'clock tomorrow afternoon?"

The answer was another body blow to his ego. "I don't think you understand me. How about one hour from now – and no staff present?"

"What the hell is going on here, why are…….."

The AG interrupted him with "You want to be re-elected President, then I suggest you clear your desk and see me in one hour."

"I don't know what the hell this is all about, but it better be good."

"It is. I'll see you in 58 minutes."

The President hung up and thought to himself "If I do manage to get re-elected he is going to be the first one to walk the plank. He can't talk to me like that and get away with it."

****

Exactly one hour later Aaron Freedman, the Attorney General of the United States, was directed into the Oval Office. The President's Chief of Staff was sitting in one of the chairs facing the desk, and as the AG neared the desk he turned to the Chief of Staff, and said, "Would you please excuse us for a few minutes?"

The President started to bluster "He works for me and he can hear anything......"

The Attorney General repeated his request and turned to the President and said, "I told you that this was to be a private meeting."

"Okay, okay! You sound more like you're working for the CIA than for me "....but then he turned and nodded for the Chief of Staff to leave the room.

Once they were alone, the AG chose to totally ignore the agitated state that the President was in and he said, "I received a call last night from one of our Federal Attorneys in Texas. He was contacted by the Mayor of El Paso who is prepared to blow the whistle on Bobby Houston on Monday."

"Blow the whistle about what?" as the President began to sense the reason for all of the urgency and secrecy behind this meeting.

The AG briefly described the conversation with Rodrique Castillo and the fact that the Mayor had a tape of his conversation with Bobby Houston.

"Holy shit! If we blow this up, it will ruin Houston, and no elector in their right mind will vote for him. Maybe with a bunch of his votes along with mine we could get pretty close. What did you tell him?"

"I told him I wanted to go over the situation with my staff and that I would get back to him this morning. I didn't tell him that I was going to go directly to you, although he is pretty damn savvy, and I suspect he knows exactly what I will be doing."

"So what's our next step?"

"The Mayor is going to leak a news story after the markets close on Friday, alerting all the networks and a lot of other media that he is resigning immediately and will address the public on Monday morning. He wants our guy to join him at the Press Conference."

"Better yet," the President interjected "Why don't *you* join both of them? Let's make a big splash about how seriously we take the election process and how dedicated we are to law and order, blah, blah, blah. Is there anything else we can do to really smack his ass hard?"

"Well, I was thinking of announcing that we were calling a special Federal Grand Jury to consider the criminal implications of what we have just learned to really show how serious we are about the whole matter."

"Good, good, good! I like that. We'll totally humiliate that pompous red neck, as well as get a whole lot of electoral votes at the same time. God, this is just too good! I don't suppose we have anything on Worthington, do we?"

The Attorney General waited for the President to quit rubbing his hands together and literally salivating at the prospect of destroying one of his two opponents in the election which had yet to be decided.

"There is one other thing, and that is primarily the reason I wanted this meeting to be private."

The President looked up with a puzzled look on his face and said "So what other juicy tidbit to you have for me. I'm liking you more and more the longer you keep talking!"

"Well, you may not like this so much. I also received a call last night from someone I would rather not identify, who filled me in on a phone call which was supposedly made from this office on Wednesday morning, regarding the absentee ballots in Chicago."

"And just what did this 'mysterious caller' have to say, exactly?" as the President's eyes bore directly into the eyes of the Attorney General.

Well, let's just say that if that conversation should get to the street, it would put you in exactly the same position that Bobby Houston finds himself in today. Did you make the phone call that my informant tells me you did?"

The Attorney General was extremely uncomfortable as the President seemed to squirm in his seat as he considered his response."Well, I may have gotten a little excited, but I certainly didn't mean for the Mayor to do anything wrong, no, no, no I certainly didn't try to make anything illegal happen."

"Could Backstrom have taped your conversation?"

The President went totally ashen. "Oh, God, you don't think he might have done *that*, do you?"

"I think that is exactly what he may have done and what is worse, he and the Mayor appear to have gone into hiding shortly after you had that conversation. I tried to reach the mayor's office last night and I was told that the Mayor had decided to take a few days off to an unidentified destination where it would be very difficult to reach him! As for Backstrom I have no idea where he is. And the fact of the matter is they both may have tapes of their conversations."

The President slumped back in his chair, and then very weakly said, "If either of those tapes comes to light, I'll be ruined every bit as much as Houston. I don't think they could impeach me because there is hardly enough time to do that, unless.........."

"Unless they heard about it in the next few days and started proceedings immediately. So, I think we should just forge ahead with the attack on Bobby Houston, and put a full court-press spin on how dedicated we are to law and order and how much we frown on activity such as that happening in Texas. I will continue to try and reach Backstrom and the Mayor. I'll also get a few FBI guys to discreetly look for both of them. I do know a couple of people pretty high up in the mayor's administration and I'll see if I can't reach him that way. Then we'll do whatever we have to do to try and keep both of them quiet."

He then looked at the President and said "You did make the call, didn't you?"

"No, I actually didn't. We were sitting here talking about the election and I called Wally Backstrom and told him to make the call. So if there is a tape, it would be Wally Backstrom who has it."

"Anyone else in the room we should be concerned about?"

"Yeah, I got pretty excited, and when that young snot-nosed kid Jeremiah Brady started telling me how unpopular I was all around the country, I fired him on the spot. Kicked his ass right out of here!"

"So, it's safe to say, he's a bit disgruntled, to put it mildly?"

"I suppose so, but if he knows what's good for him, he'll keep his mouth shut."

"Well, I beg to disagree with you on that one. He could probably sell that story to the Enquirer for more than he would make in a year here, so keeping quiet may not be something that will be very attractive to a young guy like him. I'll try to track him down too and see if I can convince him to keep quiet!

"Do you have any more to tell me about this, or do I have it all now?"

"No, I think you have it all. I can't believe that we got such a great break with Houston's screw-up, and now…I just don't know. I don't want to lose this opportunity. How difficult do you think it will be to fix this thing?

"Frankly your goddamn attitude is blowing my mind! You still don't get it, do you? You used the phone to call Wally Backstrom (who probably taped the call) screaming at him to fix the vote in Chicago, and then you fire Brady for having the temerity to tell you to your face what everyone else has been saying behind your back. Then Backstrom undoubtedly calls the Mayor of Chicago (who also probably taped the call) and he repeats what you ordered him to do. You have created a real strong case for some investigator to determine that you were trying to fix an election by ordering a subordinate (or more than one) to break the law. So if you don't like my attitude, then just fire me right now and get some other lackey in here who doesn't care if he gets indicted. I was tempted to bring in my resignation this morning anyhow, but then for some reason that escapes me right now, I thought better of it. I was kind of hoping that you would tell me that this never happened. But I guess, from all the smoke, I knew there had to be plenty of fire!"

The President sat slumped in his chair. He was seething at what Aaron Freedman had just said to him. So he decided that he would not even acknowledge the Attorney General's last comments.

The President looked up at Freedman. He thought to himself "You are so damned smart aren't you? So smart, so clever. Got yourself picked as Attorney General and you're only 40 something. Well, see how this shoe fits Mr.Smart-ass lawyer.

"How much will it cost? I can get you five million dollars by tonight – will that be enough to shut up Backstrom, and that punk Brady? Then how much to stifle the Mayor of Chicago. One phone call and I'll have the money for you tonight!"

By this time the President was sounding not only desperate, but almost hysterical.

"You know, Mr. President, I really don't know if I *can* fix it. I will try, but I'll tell you right now, I'm not going to do something that ends up putting me in jail. Believe me, I am no John Mitchell! I'll do the best that I can to keep your reputation in tact until January 20th, but I'll be damned if I'm lying for you and getting us both sent to Federal prison! But go ahead and see if you can get the money. Ten million might be enough, I just don't know. We'll have to see….."

The President picked up on Freedman's willingness to consider the money approach to solving the problem. "How do you want me to get it to you? It'll have to be in small bills won't it? I know what I'll do. I'll put it in a suitcase and have my Secretary deliver it to a long term locker at Dulles. Then she'll go to your house in Georgetown, deliver the key to you, then you run with it from there. That'll work, won't it? No one will know what is in it, or who it's for, but you'll have the money and you can do whatever you have to do with it. But you will have to let me know if it's enough. I'll get you more if we have to!"

Chapter 14

News people all around the country were stunned on Friday afternoon after the election when all three major television networks, CNN, Fox, CSPAN, the editors of fifty of the largest and most influential newspapers in the country and radio news networks nation-wide were all alerted to be prepared for a major news announcement. The message was brief but clear.

"Mayors from three of the ten largest cities in Texas simultaneously released press releases today that they were resigning from their offices immediately "for personal reasons." They also announced that they would be appearing together on Monday morning at a news conference on the steps of City Hall in San Antonio to further elaborate on the reasons behind their unprecedented actions.

The phone lines to the offices of all three of these mayors were bursting with calls, but all of the offices were already closed for the weekend so all anyone got was either a busy signal or a recorded message that the offices were closed.

There were a few local reporters who had access to phone numbers of certain high level officials in the various offices, but even that proved to be a dead end, as all of those phones offered up busy signals only.

All of the TV news stations in each of the three cities immediately dispatched their mobile units with key reporters to the homes of the mayors, but much to their disappointment, they discovered the Mayors and their families had all seemingly disappeared.

By Saturday afternoon reporters, film crews, talking heads, political analysts from all over the United States began arriving at San Antonio International Airport. Not quite as obvious was the fact that several representatives from the United States Attorney General's office along with a number of Federal Bureau of Investigation agents also made their way through the exit doors into waiting cars.

Chapter 15

Aaron Freedman had come to the White House out of the Chicago political machine with the former President. In the nearly four years that he served as Attorney General he had followed the party line on nearly all of the important issues, but he was careful not to go "over the line".

Freedman had grown up in a secure middle class home on the North side of Chicago where both of his parents were professional people. His Dad was a very successful Doctor at the Northwestern University Medical Center and his Mother was a long time High School Teacher. The fact that his father was black and his mother white never seemed to be an issue as he went through school. He knew that he was fortunate that mixed race marriages were far more acceptable in the 21st century than they had ever been 50 or 75 years earlier.

He graduated with honors at the University of Illinois and was a member of the Law Review at the University of Chicago Law School from where he was recruited into a large and highly respectable law firm in Chicago. It was only natural for him to dabble in local politics and although his firm had very deep ties to the Republican Party they were only too happy to have this smart, good looking young lawyer making a name for himself with the Daley political machine. It was just good business for firms like his to have connections on both sides of the aisle. They were justifiably proud when the Clinton administration had selected him to be a Federal Attorney in Chicago where he continued to distinguish himself, particularly with his anti-trust work. He married a high school teacher introduced to him by his mother and they were comfortably settled into an apartment on the near North side of Chicago.

Then the election in 2008 came and he was selected by the new President to be the Attorney General at the tender age of thirty-nine.

He and his wife rented a nice, but rather small home in the toney Georgetown section of Washington and he immersed himself in the affairs of the Justice Department where he was quickly recognized as an extraordinarily hard working, no-nonsense manager. The President, as most Presidents do, had his own Legal Counsel, so Aaron Freedman didn't find himself having to give personal legal advice to the President who brought him to Washington. But then with the sudden and totally unexpected death of the patron who had brought him to prominence, he suddenly had to deal with an entirely different type of leader, who was obviously not particularly fond of him.

As he returned home on Thursday after his meeting with the President he was in an extremely agitated mood. His wife, Pamela Martin Freedman met him at the door and could sense that he was upset.

"What's up Aaron? You look terrible! What's going on?"

He proceeded to tell her about most of the conversation in the Oval Office that morning.

He took the glass of wine she poured for him and said, "The President is in complete denial. He just doesn't understand or maybe doesn't care how reckless his actions have been, and he sure doesn't understand the real danger he and this administration are in right now!"

Pamela was twirling the Merlot in her glass very slowly, and she said "Are you okay? I mean are you in trouble too?"

"You know, up until the last few minutes of our meeting this morning, I was doing fine. I had received a call that told me what happened Wednesday morning, and I tried like hell to get hold of Wally Backstrom and the Mayor of Chicago, but they've just disappeared. But I will get to them, believe me I will get to them. I've got the Director of the FBI himself working on finding those two. And I did what I would expect any responsible Attorney General to do – I went to the President with what I found out."

He paused and took a sip of his wine, as his wife studied his face.

She said, "But something else happened. What was it?"

"Well, I hoped that he would tell me that the whole thing didn't happen or at least didn't happen the way I heard it. But, he didn't say that - he sort of sloughed it off as just an example of how he 'gets excited" some times. But I challenged him. I said it did happen didn't it? And he admitted it. But that's where it really gets messy, and where I'm right in the middle of this toilet bowl."

"My God, what did he say to you?"

"He asked me to 'fix it'! He wants it fixed and he wants it to go away. I told him I wasn't sure that I *could* fix it and that is where the story gets really weird!"

"Honey, you aren't a fixer! Not in Chicago and certainly not in Washington. How are you supposed to fix something that sounds really illegal to me.? What does he think you are? Some kind of magician?”

“He asked me how much money it would take to ‘take care of Backstrom and the Mayor’.

“Oh, no! He didn’t really say that did he?”

“Oh, yes! I’m afraid he did say that.”

“Then what?”

“I wasn’t honestly sure that he was serious, but then he said he could get $5,000,000 by tonight. In small bills no less! So I made a quick decision. I told him it would probably take $10,000,000 and he said that was no problem. He said he would put the money in a suit case and have his secretary deliver it to a locker at Dulles tonight and then she’ll drop the key off to me here – tonight!”

“Aaron, are you making this up?”

“No, I wish I was. I told him I was not going to lie for him and I sure wasn’t going to do anything that put me or him in jail, but that didn’t stop him for a minute. He is in total denial, total denial.”

“What a mess! What *are* you going to do?”

“Well for starters, I asked Mitch Robertson, who is an Assistant Attorney General and a holdover from the last administration – and by the way, a very straight shooter – to do two things for me. First of all he is having the President’s secretary followed when she leaves the White House tonight – to confirm that she drops the bag at Dulles. He will recover the bag in the locker and see that it is secured at FBI headquarters. Then he is coming over here about seven o'clock tonight and he is going to be here along with another Federal attorney to witness her dropping off the key."

"And?"

"Well, first of all when she arrives here with the key, just pretend like nothing is out of the ordinary. You know, ask her how her kids are, and all that stuff. We don't want to alarm her.

"And then sweet love of my life, I suggest you tune in to the News Conference from San Antonio on Monday morning. I don't know, did I mention that he wants me to be there when we blow the whistle on the illegal activities of Bobby Houston?"

＊＊＊＊＊＊＊＊＊＊＊＊＊＊＊＊＊＊＊＊＊

The two men from the Attorney General's staff arrived at the Freedman house around 7pm and around 8 the door bell rang. Pam went to the door and let Marcia Marston in. After a few personal greetings and inquiries Pam led Marcia back to the family room where there were now three people seated: Aaron and two other gentlemen that Marcia didn't know.

Marcia was a single 60 year old and had been a professional secretary since she left school at 18. She had been in the White House for four years and was widely respected and liked by everyone, with the possible exception of the President for whom she had worked the last six years.

When she saw the group who by now were all politely standing, Marcia became highly alarmed and now a little agitated. She kind of mumbled, "I'm sorry am I interrupting some kind of meeting. I really don't want to break into your party or whatever. I just have an envelope to deliver to you Mr. Freedman. I think you are expecting it."

Aaron responded "Marcia, you are not interrupting anything. Is this the key to the locker at Dulles?"

"Yes, it is."

"And the President asked you to deliver this key to me?"

"Yes, he did. Mr. Freedman I am getting really bad vibes about this whole thing. Am I in some sort of trouble?"

One of the two gentlemen in the room then asked "Ms. Marston, do you know what was in the suitcase you dropped off at the airport?"

"May I ask who you are?"

Aaron spoke up saying "I am sorry Marcia for being so rude. These two fellas are both assistant attorney generals, and they work out of my office."

"What's this all about Mr. Freedman? Please tell me if I am in some kind of trouble. Doing this thing tonight seemed so strange to me. But in answer to your question, no, I don't have a clue what was in that suitcase. He just said it was 'a little something' for Mr. Freedman."

"Well, Marcia. That little suitcase contains $10,000,000 which the President wants me to use to guarantee that he wins the vote in Illinois. How does that sound to you?"

Marcia virtually collapsed into one of the side chairs as the tears began to pour down her cheeks. "Oh, my God, I swear to you that I didn't know what was in there. Oh, my God! Oh, my God! What do I do now?"

"Marcia, these men are going to go home with you and we want you to pack up a few things and we are going to provide you with a safe place to live for the next couple of weeks. You will have to call in tomorrow morning and simply say that you have had an emergency come up in your family and that you will be gone for a few days. Can you do that?"

Through a face covered with tears Marcia looked up and said, "Yes, I can do that, but please tell me that I'm not in some kind of trouble. Please?"

"Marcia, you are not in trouble, but I'm not sure that I can say the same for your boss."

Chapter 16

NBC news was the first to break the story around 11am on Sunday when one of its local reporters in Austin, Texas announced that the Board of Elections in Texas had finally completed the counting of the absentee ballots and was ready to announce the final results of the voting in Texas. A press conference was scheduled for Monday morning around 10am which was immediately preceding the highly anticipated News/ Press Conference which would supposedly feature the three Mayors, or their representatives.

The representative from the State Election Board stated that he was not authorized to reveal the results of the balloting until given the go-ahead by the Governor, but the Governor had abruptly left town for parts unknown and so the representative said that by law he would have to wait until Monday morning when he would announce the results with or without the Governor's blessing.

The Press that had gathered to hear this announcement then began firing questions at the rather innocuous looking state official, who was obviously uneasy about the position he was in.

"Where is the Governor?" was the question everyone shouted at almost the same time.

"I really don't know. You can ask me twenty times if you want, but I do not know. I called his office late yesterday and I got some clerical person or other and she said that she wasn't authorized to reveal where the Governor was, and then she also said, authorized or not, she did not know where he was, and then she said she didn't know anyone who does know. Just before she hung up she said have you tried his ranch? "

"Did someone get enough votes to win all the electoral votes?" came a question from a reporter from CNN.

"I am not authorized to reveal the results at this time" was the answer.

"Is Bobby back in his Austin office?" shouted a Reuters reporter.

"How many times do I have to tell you? I don't know where he is."

"Who did you speak to at the Governor's office?"

"Well, that's kind of strange, too. She refused to tell me who she was, and when I called back a few minutes later, the line was busy. So I never found out."

"Don't you think that is kind of peculiar?"

"Yes, I would say that is 'peculiar' as you call it. But, I don't pretend to understand how politics works; I just help run elections!"

"Do you think the Governor has suffered some kind of foul play?"

"Folks, how the hell do I know what is going on with the Governor? I'm here for one reason. To tell the world that the vote counting in Texas is over and by law I will announce the results tomorrow morning at 10am! Okay? Thanks for your time."

With that final comment the Election official turned his back on the pack of howling reporters and disappeared into a white SUV and sped away from the scene.

The reporters backed off and then began calling their employers and reporting what they had just heard. Of course the editors and publishers back at their respective companies were simply not satisfied and they all quickly went into huddles to determine just how far they wanted to go in pursuit of the mystery of the missing Governor, the missing Mayors and their families and the as yet unaccounted for ballot results.

In the end most of them decided that there really wasn't much they could do at this point, but those who had not already authorized a reporter to go to San Antonio, hastily dug up the top reporter that they had available and dispatched that person to Texas that afternoon.

At virtually the same time all of the reporters tried to call out to the Governor's Ranch, several media groups dispatched their mobile trucks to the area of the Ranch. To their disappointment there were already several news agencies already positioned outside the gates of the Ranch, and they all reported the same thing. There had been absolutely no sign of the Governor, nor his family, nor any of his fairly large office and campaign staff. So, they all just hunkered down to wait just in case he came careening out of the Ranch in the next few hours.

Chapter 17

It was a slightly overcast day this Monday after the national election....rather unusual for San Antonio for early in November. There had been a buzz around town that reached a deafening roar by Sunday morning when virtually every Church in town heard some kind of sermon, homily or simply words of wisdom regarding the announcement about their Mayor on Friday. The speculation was rife.

Just why had this popular and up and coming young politician chosen to abruptly resign his office – and more mystifying than that was the simultaneous announcements that the mayors of, El Paso, and Plano had also resigned as well! *The San Antonio News, The Dallas Morning News* and *The El Paso Times* all had virtually the same bold faced headline:

WHAT'S GOING ON?

The clergy were all pretty well convinced that these leading politicians from all across the state had all been caught in some kind of illegal undertaking probably having to do with the ever present illegal immigration and drug smuggling operations that were going on just across the border in Mexico. They were all theorizing that no matter what the issue or issues were, it had to come down to God finally saying "Enough already! This all has to stop!" and then through some form of divine intervention these resignations were brought about and heaven only knew what was to follow.

The local Press was totally baffled, and all the more so because all three Mayors had virtually disappeared – with their families! Conspiracy theorists were having a field day. They concluded that it was perfectly obvious that these three (and perhaps others) were up to their eye-balls in some kind of nefarious enterprise – probably related to drugs, and the cartel had concluded that they were going to turn states witness and blow the whole enterprise. So, good luck to the law enforcement people who were looking high and low for these guys: they and their families were long ago buried in a barrel full of highly toxic lye somewhere far out on the desert.

The Governor's office was abnormally quiet about the whole affair considering the fact that Governor Bobby Houston would ordinarily have jumped on something like this with both feet, both arms and his entire face. This was a photo-opportunity extraordinaire and Bobby never missed a chance to get his face on the wide screen. But all that came from the Governor's office was that one of his people had ordered the state police to look into the matter and see if they could determine what had happened to the three men and their families.

With that announcement, and the fact that the Governor himself was also nowhere to be found, the plot seemed to get even thicker. Perhaps the Governor was also involved with this international cartel and the smuggling ring which they managed. Perhaps the Governor and his family were also cremated on the desert floor somewhere! So, **WHAT WAS GOING ON?**

Chapter 18

There are places on the Jersey shore that are both beautiful and isolated. Walking early in the morning in the first half of November can be dicey at best. But fortunately for Senator Ellen Livingston the area was virtually deserted, unlike what it is like during the summer when every Tom, Dick and Harry from Connecticut south descends on the area. It took them a couple of hours to get here, but as far as clearing your head in the unbelievably refreshing salt air – there was just nothing like it.

She had left her companion for the evening sleeping peacefully while she quickly slipped into her warm jogging clothes. She particularly welcomed the hood to protect her ears from the cool breeze blowing in off the Atlantic this morning. She had stolen away from the election party around 10pm when it appeared that Mark Worthington was all but elected. She figured a 30 minute jog would be enough this morning to get her body functions in proper running order and then she could return to the room and catch the latest on the election. Hopefully it would all be over except for the last hurrahs!

She had won another term in Congress as had her long time friend and confidant, the Senator from Wisconsin Robert Madison. Her feelings for Bob had grown substantially over the last couple of years. And now over the last few months they had become lovers. The whole world knew that they were good friends and frequently dined together when Congress was in session, but so far to their knowledge no one had discovered their little secret.

As she walked the beach she thought about what would be in store for her, and Bob as well, when Congress got back in session in a few weeks. An independent President should be in the White House with the remnants of the Democrats on the left and a similarly disarrayed group of Republicans on the right, and a precious handful of us in the middle who actually declared for him and the Independence Party. "Wow!" she thought "But, how is that going to play out? Will Bob finally declare as an Independent and sit in the middle of the Senate with her, or will he stick with the Democrats? What will happen to the other 10 of us, geez, it will only be the other eight now since Luke and Harrison were defeated. It would sure help if they all declared themselves Independents, if not Independence Party independents. But will they have the cajones to do that? I don't know. Maybe I'll ask Bob this morning. But maybe I won't either. What's going to happen to our relationship now? I really think I'm falling in love with this guy. I never thought I would fall in love again – but I really like Bob! Come on girl, you know it's more than 'like' – you've fallen in love with the guy!

"Listen to me. I sound like a teen-ager talking about her new boy friend, the Captain of the football team! But it's exciting! It really is! I get kind of tingly all over when I think about him. What the hell am I doing out here on this cold, windy beach when I could be cuddled up with him in that big king-sized bed back at the Hotel? Crap! Girl, get a move on it and get back upstairs to your man, and stop just thinking about it. Do something about it!"

About ten minutes later, Ellen quietly let herself into the suite and made her way to the bathroom outside the door of their bedroom. She quickly got out of her jogging clothes and looked at herself in the mirror. "Not too bad for an old broad" she thought to herself. She quickly brushed her hair back into place and then slipped off the rest of her clothes and moved into the bedroom where Bob appeared to be peacefully sleeping on his side. She crawled in behind him and put her hands around his waist and drew herself up tightly behind him.

With that move Bob was thoroughly aroused, and realizing what was happening he turned over and brought her tightly into his arms. He said, "I heard you come into the room, and I was hoping you would do this."

He touched her face and whispered, "I love you Ellen Livingston! Would you consider marrying me? I want to sweep you off your feet and take you back to Wisconsin where we'll become cheese-heads and live happily ever after!"

Ellen said, "Tell you what. I promise that I will think about it but right now what I want is more of you and less talking for a little while." She kissed him with a long and loving kiss and they just held each other before they both fell asleep again.

****

It was well past 11am when Ellen woke to the smell of fresh coffee brewing. Bob was up and pouring a cup for her. She sat up in bed, and holding the cup in both hands she looked up at him and said, "Now, I'd really like to hear more about how a Jersey Girl becomes a cheese-head!"

Bob Madison laughed quietly, saying "Ellen I really meant what I said. I want to marry you. Will you consider that?"

"I will consider it, and honestly, right now I'm almost tempted to say let's do it, and go find a Justice of the Peace and get it done! But, then my more cautious side says, slow down girl. We have an awful lot to consider here. I'm a Senator Bob – and so are you. We're from different states, different parties. We have big responsibilities that we have to consider. We have constituencies to consider. There is just so much to think about1"

Ellen then got up and moved over to where Bob was sitting on a stool at the kitchen counter. "But, Bob, believe me. I love you, too! I just think we need to consider all of the implications. I don't know? This isn't just two people in love who want to bring their lives together. Am I making any sense at all?"

Bob took her hands in his and said, "Of course you are making sense. You are one of the most sensible people I have ever met. Frankly, I have always thought it was a bit of a miracle that someone as sensible as you could ever get elected to our holy body. But you did! And you are a great Senator. No offense meant to Mark Worthington but I still think you would have been a great candidate for President, and would have made a great President! But yes, you are right. We do have to consider all of the issues that would come up to complicate our lives. But, I'll tell you what. I want to marry you Ellen. And I want it badly enough, that I'll leave the Senate if that will smooth the way! So, I'm taking what you just said as a Yes! And that makes me about the happiest guy in America today!"

Bob then gave Ellen a big hug and another kiss, and said "To start with we'll just keep our little secret a secret a bit longer while we sort all of this out. Does that make you feel a little better?"

"You always say the nicest things Mr. Madison. It does make me feel better, and who says that *you* have to leave your Senate seat? Maybe I should leave mine. Maybe I'll reconsider some conversations I had with Mark Worthington a few weeks ago. Yes, indeed, I may just reconsider one of his offers.

The attention of both of them was drawn to the television screen when one of the national commentators began talking about the surprise announcement out of Texas about the resignations of the three Mayors, on top of the possibility of the Presidential election being thrown into the House of Representatives. It was then they realized just how complicated their lives might actually become in the next few months.

Chapter 19

As Jeff Corcoran walked from his car to his Capitol Hill office his head was swirling with thoughts about what this day might bring to everyone in this country. It was Monday after his re-election, but it was no run of the mill Monday. The final election results were due this morning from Maryland, Illinois and Texas, and there was so much left to be decided from the previous week's election. His man and his new Party won the most votes for President and that was set in stone, no matter what happened in these three late-counters. But the electoral count was still up for grab, and he thought to himself "God knows which way those three states may go", and as yet Mark was just a little short of having the 270 votes necessary for outright election.

Then his brow furrowed as he wondered what he hell was going on in San Antonio this morning. Well, he and his staff were prepared to watch that show, whatever it was all about.

As he stepped through the door into the outer office of his suite he was greeted by his staff all of whom were anxious to let him know just how much they had missed him. Coffee and donuts for everyone sat on the side table, and everyone began congratulating him regarding his re-election and especially for the part he had played in Worthington's stunning victory!

His administrative assistant assured them all that she had picked up low fat rolls only! But, no one believed that for even a second.

After making the rounds and shaking everyone's hand and giving hugs to all the female staffers, Jeff quieted everyone down and said "I can't tell you all how happy I am to be back home. You all have done an absolutely fabulous job of keeping this office together and humming like I hadn't even been out of town. Come to think of it, that's a little scary, isn't it? You all told me that you missed me, but seeing how well the office ran with me gone, one really has to wonder about just how important *is* the guy with the big desk!"

A chorus of "No, no, no's" rippled through the room, and Jeff laughed right along with them. "Well, just because you did so well without me, doesn't mean that I'm going to give up this cushy job and go back to the Insurance business in Ohio! So, for the next six years you'll just have to get used to having me around!

"But on a more serious note, this really has been a special time for me, and more so for our country. A third party candidate winning an election is about as historic as elections get, and it looks like Mark is right on the edge of making that a reality. I understand we'll get the final vote counts in an hour or so, so say a little, prayer, maybe keep your fingers and toes crossed, or whatever you do for good luck. It would be a crying shame if he doesn't win this thing outright.

"I will tell you all this much though. I have been privileged to be very close to Mark Worthington these past several months, and he is very much a special person. One way or another I think he is going to be our next President, and I can't wait for that day to come, because I think he is going to be a very special President! So, thank you for helping me get elected again, and for taking care of this office while I was campaigning and also helping a truly great man get elected (at least I hope he is going to be elected). You have all done a wonderful job, and now I'm anxious to get back to work.

"On a more serious note, this election represents a very challenging turning point in our history. And we – you - I are all right in the eye of this storm. For the first time in the modern history of our country we are going to have three, not two, but three very distinct political parties on the floor of the Senate and on the floor of the House of Representatives. The issues that this will raise are significant if not a little mind-boggling. So, over the next few days I am going to ask you to do a lot of research and a lot of thinking as to how we proceed, so that we can make this work for the good of the country. The picture is unclear right now and the task before us – and all of the rest of the Senators and Representatives - is an enormously difficult one. But, I am confident that we can and will figure it out and that our country and our government will be better and stronger due to our collective efforts. Are you excited?"

All of the staff members took a second to let all of this sink in when they started clapping and laughing and in one form or another let Jeff know that he could count on them to do everything possible to make the transition to the new government a smooth and successful one.

With all of that said, Mark beckoned his Chief of Staff to join him in his office where the television was already turned on to the News Conference out of San Antonio.

J. Peter Morgan, his chief of staff settled in the easy chair in front of Jeff's desk. Jeff liked to tell people he hired Pete because he always admired people who went by their middle name and signed everything with a first initial and middle name. Pete Morgan was just a little over thirty and had moved from running his Ohio office to Washington when Jeff had fired Chad Denson. Pete had no hidden agendas like Chad had had, and he quickly became adjusted to the frenetic pace of running a

Senator's office in Washington. Like Chad Denson before him he was single. But, unlike Chad, he was not a shy policy wonk, but rather a bit of a man about town. He enjoyed a very active social life and was routinely kidded about the harem he was reported to control in and around the District of Columbia.

Pete started their conversation with the question that was on everyone's mind in Washington "What the hell is going on down there?"

"So, you think because I'm a Senator that I should know?" was Jeff's response.

"Well, no, I suppose not, except there is something really funny about this whole thing. Three large city mayors quitting a day or two after the election, and then they disappear with their families? And now I understand that Bobby Houston has also gone missing. Is this some kind of Election-Day Massacre, you know like the old Valentine's Day massacre in Chicago?"

"Honestly, Pete, I don't know anymore than you do, but I seriously doubt there's been a massacre! There is certainly something sinister about the whole series of events, but I have a hunch that most or all of them are going to show up in a few minutes and we'll have an answer to this whole thing.

"But, in the meantime there is something I want you to get a couple of your people started on. I want all the information you can dig up about what happens when an election goes into the House. If Mark doesn't win either Illinois or Texas, we are going to have one Constitutional mess on our hands. Then have one of the interns prepare a short white paper outlining the count in the House, and in the Senate, so that we can get some sense of how this thing might play out if no one gets enough of those electoral votes.

"In the meantime, are there any other issues you need to bring me up to speed on? I'm sure hoping there are only a couple!"

Chapter 20

The President finished his morning briefings well before the scheduled Press Conference in San Antonio. He called in his chief of staff and three of his top domestic political advisors to join him as the time approached for the news conference. The staff was surprised when Martin DuPont Remington III, an old Washington legal hand and the President's personal lawyer joined the group. Remington was a senior member of the venerable Washington Law firm once known as Wilmer Cutler Pickering Hale and Dorr. His law firm had a long history of serving Presidents as legal counselors, as well as performing many other formal and informal functions for many residents of the White House.

The other three all greeted Remington cordially, but there had already been a couple of quiet comments exchanged between them as to why Remington had been invited to watch this San Antonio news conference. The President appeared to be very at ease and so he opened the conversation with a few background comments.

"For your information fellas, the Attorney General got wind of some funny things going on down in Texas with regard to the very large number of uncounted absentee ballots as well as some unconfirmed rumors surrounding the Governor's office with regard to those ballots. Aaron and his staff are aggressively tracking down all the loose ends relating to what he heard. And by the way Martin, Aaron reported those rumors to me almost immediately.

"As you all know, this administration is totally, 100% committed to upholding the laws of this country and if there was any criminal activity whatsoever in Texas we are pledged to do everything in our power to indict, and to prosecute those who are responsible. And I might add, that would include that bastard Bobby Houston!"

Martin Remington looked out over his reading glasses and addressing the President said, "From what you have just said, it sounds like there must be a lot of smoke down there. Do you really think there is also some fire? And by the way, where is Aaron this morning? I would have expected him to be sitting in on this meeting."

The President shifted slightly in his chair so that he could look Remington directly in the eyes. "Good question, Martin. Aaron is in San Antonio as we speak. As you may have heard, the three mayors who are supposed to speak today have not been heard from in several days, and there are real concerns for their safety. But as a matter of fact nobody has heard from Bobby Houston either, so I personally directed that Aaron go down there himself and do what has to be done to get to the bottom of this mystery and to guarantee the sanctity of all those absentee ballots!

"Aaron has had the Justice Department and the FBI on this all weekend and I am confident that he will break the case very soon. I know that he intends to speak at the news conference, but I guess we'll just have to wait to see what he has come up with so far."

Remington quietly turned to the others in the room and addressing them as a group said, "It sounds like the Attorney General has this situation well in hand. However, there is something about this whole scenario that is just not sitting right with me. Maybe it is just my natural doubting nature, but is there anything out there that I don't know about that could come back to bite us in the ass?"

The President quickly answered for the group. "No, no, I don't know of anything that would adversely affect us. But I do think that Bobby Houston may have a lot of 'splaining to do!"

Remington went back to his notes, and thought to himself, "Why did he feel that he had to answer that question, *and* answer it that fast? There is something I don't know about? But what is it?"

****

Meanwhile, Aaron Freedman had arrived in San Antonio. He took an afternoon flight on Sunday, and was met at the airport by two of the Justice Department attorneys, one from the El Paso area and one from San Antonio. They immediately were driven to a Hotel not too far from the city offices where the Press Conference was scheduled for Monday.

Aaron was quite familiar with Oscar Ramirez the attorney from the San Antonio office, but had had only a brief encounter with Jordan Jackson a couple of years earlier.

"So, tell me what you know so far" as he looked at Oscar Ramirez.

"Well, sir…"

"Please call me Aaron, guys. I much prefer being on a first name basis than all that sir stuff. Okay?"

Oscar smiled broadly, and continued "Well, Aaron, sir, I just don't know a whole lot at this point. But to sum up what I do know: sometime early Wednesday morning it's alleged that the Governor placed a number of calls to Mayors in the state, including one to the Mayor of San Antonio and another to the Mayor of El Paso The Mayor of El Paso called me a day or so later and told me that the Governor sounded like he was very angry and highly agitated. He threatened the Mayor by telling him if he didn't do what the Governor told him to do, that he - the Governor – would ruin him politically. He said get into those absentee ballots and make damn sure the vote comes out for me – no matter what you have to do!"

Aaron Freedman was making notes on a long yellow legal pad, and at this point he looked up at Oscar and said, "Was there more?"

"Yeah, there was one more item. He called the Mayor a 'slimey wetback' and that if he didn't do as directed, he'd be back 'picking cotton' somewhere next year."

"Jesus God almighty! A slimy wetback'? What was he thinking? Do we have any way to corroborate all this?"

Oscar Ramirez answered "Well, we actually have two things. We have the tape recording of the conversation that the Mayor is holding, and that we have listened to. It's not the greatest recording I ever heard, but it is clear enough. Then we have what Jordan here learned at close to the same time I spoke to the Mayor. Tell him your story Jordan."

"Well, as it turns out, the Mayor of El Paso decided immediately that he wasn't going to play ball, so he called a number of other mayors from some of the larger cities in Texas, and asked them if anyone had contacted them to maybe try and fix the outcome of the election. He couldn't reach a couple of them, but he hit pay dirt here with the Mayor of San Antonio. Since the guy here was kind of evasive with his answers Castillo got pretty aggressive with my guy, and finally he admitted that he had received virtually the same call, and he was scared to death – for a lot of reasons! But when he was told that the Federal attorney for El Paso had been contacted, he decided the best thing for him to do was to call me.

"He told me an almost identical story, and let me listen to his tape which turned out to be of much higher quality. The Governor's message was exactly what these two guys reported."

"Okay, then how did the other Mayor get involved? He's from Plano – right?"

"Right! He took a call from the El Paso guy and denied having been contacted. He wasn't real convincing, I guess, but Castillo accepted his denial on the surface. Then later, Plano's man reconsidered and called Castillo and confirmed that he had been called too. But, it's really interesting that the Mayor of Dallas got pretty hostile and actually hung up on him!"

"So, Dallas won't be on the platform tomorrow, I take it."

"Doesn't look like it. I have several FBI agents looking into the vote counting for Dallas to see if anything funny was happening. But I don't have a report as yet."

"What happened to these three Mayors, and their families? It sounds like they just disappeared. What do you know about that?"

Both attorneys chuckled at this question and Jordan answered "We took them away and put them in "safe houses" until tomorrow morning. You know, we are pretty good at the Witness Protection business, so it wasn't all that hard to hide 'em somewhere. Anyhow, they were scared! They were afraid the Governor might send some Texas Ranger out to put a quick bullet in their heads! "

"I should have known! Good work guys! I'm glad you did what you did. But, now for the big question. Did any of these mayors actually bite and try to fix some of the ballots?"

"We don't know yet, but of course we are looking real close at Dallas. When the announcement with the election results is made tomorrow morning, we'll have some of our best investigators looking at those results to see if there was any messing around with the ballots. We have agents targeted on about eight other large cities, but at this point we just don't know much."

"Okay, that's good enough. How about the Federal Grand Jury?"

"Oh, yes. We have contacted the foremen of two of them and alerted them that we may call them into session as early as Tuesday, so they should be prepared. We did not tell them what the issue was, however."

"Okay, here is the way we are going to play this. Jordan, since your guy actually started the ball rolling, let's let the three mayors have their say. Then Jordan you summarize the position of the Federal government and inform the public that it is highly likely we will be taking this issue to one of the standing Federal Grand Juries on Tuesday. Then you turn it over to Oscar who will confirm all that has been revealed and announce that you will be going to the Federal Grand Jury in San Antonio on Tuesday as well. Then when you are done – no questions allowed up to this point, Oscar I want you to introduce me. I will be sitting in a limo so presumably no one will know that I am anywhere around.

"I have some comments to make which I am sure you will find interesting."

"The President has to see this as a big boost for him considering the way the election has gone so far" was Jordan's comment.

"Well, let's put it this way. The President is intensely interested in what is developing!"

Chapter 21

Governor Bobby Houston and his family were also sitting around a kitchen table on Monday morning. But, they were in a rather spacious and well equipped twelve thousand square foot 'cabin' far out on the desert in West Texas. The property belonged to a very old friend of Houston who had discreetly let the Governor use the place on a couple of other occasions.

Mary Sue Houston had been Bobby's girlfriend since they were seniors in high school. She had gone off to Southern Methodist to college, but the two were never far apart for most of their college days. He picked her up one day in July after graduation, and announced that they were getting married in two weeks, whether their parents liked it or not. Since both sets of parents understood this young man very well, there was no sense in throwing up objections. So, the date was put off for a couple of additional weeks, a Church was booked, a banquet hall engaged and at age twenty two they set out on married life.

Mary Sue had not always liked the people that Bobby chose as friends, but he was good to her and to their ever growing brood of children. She thought he swore too much, and probably drank too much but he did not mess around with other women and his career blossomed early, and his income grew quite rapidly. To be perfectly honest, Bobby Houston had "friends in high places."

She looked across the table at him. The children had finished eating and were in the family room watching TV. Very quietly she said "Bobby, why are we here?"

He sensed that she knew something wasn't right. But, then how could she not know that there was something wrong with this picture? He had her pack up the kids on about 30 minutes notice the week before and they got in their SUV and drove west just before sundown. This place was several hours from Austin and except to fill up with gas, they had not stopped until they arrived at the Cabin. He had always been pretty straightforward with her during their thirty-some years of marriage, but now she asked this very honest, and to the point question. Why were they where they were?

He started by saying "Sweetheart, in politics you sometimes have to do things that later on you may not be totally proud of, but damn it, the end zone in politics is to get elected! You have to get elected! We have worked so hard this past year to get to last Tuesday……it just broke my heart to think that we may have lost the election because that sonofabitch Mark Worthington decided to go off on his own and start a third party.

"Mary Sue, we had this thing won! We had it won! We had the Presidency in our hands! We had it! Then he comes along and fucks it up for everybody! A third party – whoever would have thought something like that could possibly have happened? "

"Honey, would you please watch your language? The children are in the other room, and I know, they have heard you swear before, but I'm just not comfortable with it. Please?"

"Okay, okay, but just thinking about this whole thing just makes my blood boil!"

"But, what does the election have to do with us sneaking out of town and hiding out here – in this, this….God forsaken place?

Don't get me wrong, this is one nice cabin, but we might as well be on the moon, it's so isolated. So why are we here?"

"Well, when the news broke last Wednesday morning that the election was still up for grabs, and that the absentee vote in Texas was one of the places that was still possible to win, I got really excited!"

"And?"

"And I made a stupid bunch of phone calls, from my office."

Mary Sue had a deep frown on her face as she asked, "Who in the world did you call?"

"I called the Mayors in about ten of the biggest cities in the state, and I sort of demanded that they intercept the absentee ballots, and make damn sure that I won the State of Texas."

"I got pretty vulgar with a few of them, and I threatened to ruin all of them politically, if they didn't make sure that I won enough votes to carry the state."

"So, is this why these Mayors are having some kind of Press Conference this morning? Is this why they resigned? Because of what you said to them privately?"

"At least one of them recorded our phone conversation" and with that Bobby Houston began to cry.

Mary Sue got up and came around behind his chair and put her arms around him and held on to his shoulders. By this time he was sobbing uncontrollably. Two of the children heard him crying and they came into the room, where their Mother motioned for them to go back in the other room. They had never seen their father cry, and of course could not imagine what was wrong.

He then got some control of himself and continued "They are going to ruin me this morning – they are going to tell the world what I did, and they are going to ruin me forever!"

Mary Sue sat back down again, and holding his hands, she said, "Look at me. We still have each other. We'll get through this. So what if you are out of politics – you still have lots of friends and a law degree – you can start a new career. You are healthy, we are healthy, the kids are healthy! I'm sick of politics anyhow!"

"You don't understand. They may indict me for breaking the law. It wouldn't surprise me if they brought in the Feds to investigate this whole business. I could go to jail!"

With that said, Mary Sue also began to cry as she looked at the man she had been with almost her whole life. He was a shell of the hard charging Texan that had stormed to the top of the Republican Party and almost won the Presidency. She knew at that point that it wouldn't make any difference if he was indicted or not. He was finished, and she and the family were the only things he had left to cling to in life. She sure couldn't abandon him now, no matter how bad it got.

Mary Sue stood and said, "Let's clear the table, and get the dishes in the dishwasher and then let's go into the family room and watch the news conference from San Antonio. There is no way to hide this from the kids, so let's face it together. It could be a tough week coming up!"

Chapter 22

At 9:45 Monday morning NBC interrupted its regularly scheduled news program with a flash bulletin: "The results are in from Illinois, and the President has carried the state by the slimmest of margins. At this point, it looks like the President has about a 400 vote lead over Mark Worthington, the Independence Party candidate. Repeating, Illinois has been won by the President."

Brian Williams went on "It appears that what was a close race all night in Illinois was finally turned around in favor of the President when the last of the thousands of absentee ballots were finally counted. There were just enough votes dropped for the President that he was able to claim victory. NBC news has now officially declared that the President is a winner in Illinois – albeit by the thinnest of margins. Thin enough that a recount is undoubtedly called for. But for now, stay tuned to NBC for further news bulletins regarding Texas and Maryland which we are anticipating momentarily."

✳✳✳✳✳✳✳✳✳✳✳✳✳✳✳✳✳

Roger and Jack, the network talking heads were sitting around the conference desk with guests Henry and Richard. They were all busy preparing for the upcoming news conference in Texas. The problem they all had was they were not at all sure what was going to come out of this news conference so they were essentially going to have to wing it when they were called upon to pontificate about what they heard. This was not an ideal situation for some of them because they were much more confident when reading (from the teleprompter) comments that had been carefully crafted by writers in back rooms at the studios.

However, Roger ventured "So, Illinois has gone to the President. What exactly does that mean? Seems to me it means two things: he is still way behind in the electoral count and has no way in hell of winning the election outright; and secondly, he is counting on trying to block Mark Worthington from winning it outright, so that he might become a long shot to win it all in the House. How do you see it Jack?"

Jack was his fellow network analyst and a long time veteran observer of political campaigns. He answered "I think you've nailed it there Roger. What I am puzzled about is this situation in Texas with the missing mayors. Worthington has to win Texas to keep it out of the House, so my naturally suspicious nature is eating at the back of my brain that something is seriously wrong in Texas, or why else would these guys simply up and disappear? Does it have something to do with the election results in Texas? I'm almost more anxious to hear who won Texas than I am to hear the news conference!"

Both Peter, the longtime Democratic analyst and Henry, his counterpoint from the GOP, simply nodded their heads signaling general agreement with Jack's assessment.

Only Ernie Hardesty, the former Senator from Iowa, and a leading campaigner and supporter of Mark Worthington was willing to comment briefly on what he thought. "I think it would be a damn shame if Mark Worthington doesn't take Texas and win the whole thing today. He is far ahead in the popular vote, and so close in the electoral count – and so far ahead of the other two – it would just seem to be an injustice if he doesn't win it today. I'm also sure that as close as it was in Illinois and as close as it seems to be in Texas that there will be substantial calls to recount the ballots in both of those places, and who knows how long that will take?"

With that an associate news director stuck his head in the studio door and yelled "Heads up guys, Brian is getting ready to go back on the air with another news bulletin!"

****

Brian Williams began "This is Brian Williams with a special news bulletin concerning the vote counts in Texas and Maryland. It is reliably reported that in about 3 minutes, a representative of the Texas Election Commission will announce the results of the voting in Texas. He will declare that Governor Bobby Houston has managed to carry Texas by the very thinnest of margins with virtually all of the votes cast now having been counted. Houston is now being declared the winner in Texas by a little over 300 votes. Apparently the results from Dallas skewed the results sufficiently for the Governor to carry the state. The Elections official also announced that the Governor was currently unavailable for comment but is expected to issue a statement sometime later today.

"Election officials in Maryland reported about 10 minutes ago that Independence Party candidate Mark Worthington has been declared the winner in Maryland and will be awarded all nine electoral votes from that state. For those of you who are keeping score at home, here is how it now stands:

Worthington: 262 electoral votes

Houston: 225 electoral votes

The President 51 electoral votes

Based on this outcome, which of course is subject to change in light of how close the votes were and pending recounts in all three states, the Presidential election will now go into the House of Representatives where each state will get one vote in deciding who will be chosen President. This is an unprecedented turn of events in American politics, and of course our News Network will continue to interrupt our regularly scheduled programming to bring you up to the minute news relating to this startling development and any other related stories. Stay tuned for the upcoming news conference from San Antonio, Texas where we will be live, on scene covering this unprecedented news conference called by a group of Texas mayors who announced their abrupt resignations from office late last week."

****

The Network News Director turned the program over once again to the talking heads each of whom now had something to say, and as would be expected much of their comments reflected their personal political bias. Roger began with

"Historic! Simply historic. Totally without precedent in modern American history!"

Richard, the well respected Author and Presidential election historian commented "It is certainly without precedent over the last two hundred years, but I must caution all of you that we do still have the formality of the Electors casting their votes in the middle of December, and the Congress opening those votes and counting them in January. Then if the vote count is confirmed we will see a three ring circus like no other in recent history on the floor of the House of Representatives!"

The leading Democratic Party analyst as well as apologist, Peter offered "I think this most recent outcome certainly bodes well for the President, because the House is now split slightly in favor of the President's party, and he just might yet win his re-election bid. Wouldn't *that* be ironic?"

Henry was the Republican counter-point to Peter, and he said "Ironic? My God Peter that would be an outright travesty as far as justice is concerned. He has way less than 30% of the popular vote and way less than either of the other two candidates! How could an outcome like that be considered either fair, or equitable? I would say 'not ironic', but rather, unthinkable!"

Finally, former Senator Ernie Hardesty chimed in with "I think we had all better calm down. If this does go to the House, and some way or another, Mark Worthington is denied the Presidency, we had all better fasten our seat belts, because the Constitutional fall out from this wild ride will be heard 'round the world.'"

Richard then quietly cautioned everyone that this election was far from over. "These votes in Texas and Illinois are so close that there will be calls for substantial recounts in both of those states and the results could easily be reversed even before the Electors send in their ballots. And what about those electors? Not all of them are bound to accept the fact that they are pledged to a particular party. What if, for one reason or another 10 or 12 of those Electors pledged to the Governor, or even to the President, were to decide to switch their votes to Worthington – Election over! Worthington has a majority! So, I'd suggest that we tighten our seat belts, cause this is going to be some ride."

Chapter 23

The national media in all of their glory had arrived at the court house steps very early Monday morning and all of their mobile units were set up and ready to transmit. There were also a large number of microphones sprinkled around the court house grounds.

By 9:30 a fairly large crowd had gathered to listen to what promised to be a very interesting, and perhaps very important news conference. The reporters with access to microphones back to their studios were variously estimating the crowd to be at least one thousand up to as many as two thousand people. An impressive number of media representatives were right up front and a lot of anxious politicians and party stalwarts were not far behind. Then in the back was the usual mix of simply curious and those who hoped the panning cameras would catch them and put them on local or even national TV. There were also a few of the usual demonstrators and protestors carrying signs advocating such things as winning the war, and getting out of all wars, support Israel, support the Palestinians, outlaw abortion, support women's right to choose, eliminate the income tax, adopt a flat tax, and tax the rich, and so it went – on and on. Anything to get their faces and their signs on national television!

Then precisely at 10:00am six very long, and very black limousines with black darkened windows pulled up about 50 feet from where the news conference would be held. A number of very somber looking young men in dark suits, white shirts, and solid red ties emerged from the bowels of these super sedans and took up positions resembling what one sees when the President is in town. The people in the crowd, including the press, all turned and wondered the same thing: What was going on here?

Then one by one, the occupants of the second car began disembarking from their land cruiser. There was a woman and then a few children and finally a young man dressed in a business suit. It was then the turn for virtually the same scene from the third, and finally the fourth car. As these families adjusted to the light of a 10am sky, they began to make their way to the steps behind the bank of microphones.

Finally from the fifth and sixth cars came several more relatively young, businesslike men and women, all dressed very conservatively, with shoes polished to a mirror brilliance. These six men and women also began moving to the bank of microphones. As if moved by an unforeseen breeze, the heads in front of the crowd slowly turned as they watched this procession of people move from the sidelines to the center of their vision.

Finally one of the young men stepped to the microphone and began addressing the assembled crowd."Good morning everyone. I am Oscar Ramirez and I am the resident United States Attorney from the San Antonio office of the Justice Department of the United States. I would like to introduce you to the people who are standing behind me here. Starting on my left is the Mayor of El Paso, his wife and his children. Then to my right is the Mayor of San Antonio, who I am sure most of you out there recognize. He is joined by his wife and his children. Finally on the far right is the Mayor of Plano and his wife. Standing here beside me is another Federal attorney, Jordan Jackson who is out of our El Paso office. Finally, those folks I haven't identified are a combination of people from our respective staffs, and from the Federal Bureau of Investigation.

"You all are wondering what this meeting is all about and probably also wondering where these folks have been for the last few days. Due to the circumstances associated with the events of the last week or so, we at the Justice Department felt it was prudent to sequester all of these people for a few days in safe houses that were arranged by our department.

"Last week I received a phone call from my associate Jordan Jackson who informed me that he had been contacted by the Mayor of El Paso detailing a telephone conversation that he had had only a day or so earlier with the Governor of Texas, Governor Bobby Houston, who of course was also a candidate for President of the United States in last week's election. During this call the Governor is alleged to have directed the Mayor, in none too discreet language, to get to the absentee ballots and make sure that he, the Governor, would get most of these votes, but at the least that Mark Worthington would not get them. It is alleged that the Governor used vile and racially inappropriate language in making these demands, and he concluded by threatening to ruin the mayor politically if he did not comply with the Governor's wishes.

"At this point I am going to ask Rod Castillo, the Mayor of El Paso, if he would come forward and relate to you what he did at this point. Mayor Castillo?"

Rodrique Castillo moved slowly to the center of the bank of microphones and after introducing himself he began "To say the least, after I hung up from this call, I was pretty badly shaken up. So, I left my office and immediately went home where I told my wife what had happened. After we talked a bit I decided on my course of action. I called a number of my fellow mayors in an effort to determine if they might have received any kind of calls, similar to mine, meaning did they get a request to somehow compromise the counting of the absentee ballots in their cities. The result of my calling was somewhat mixed. I could not reach a few of the mayors, and the rest either avoided my questions or were extremely agitated that I would even suggest such a possibility. Then a few hours later the first of these two men behind me here called to let me know that he had indeed received the same type of call from the Governor.

"It was then that I decided that I had to contact Jordan Jackson, attorney for the Justice Department to let him know what had happened. I told him that I and at least two or three other Mayors would be resigning their offices that day, so that there could be no misunderstanding on anyone's part that we were having nothing to do with this incredibly bizarre scheme. Mr. Jackson then suggested that he would have the FBI come and get me and my family, as well as all of the others, and take us into protective custody for a few days. We are all indeed sorry for the anxiety we may have caused to our families, our friends, our employees, and especially to the citizens of our communities by our disappearance, but we all agreed that it was the expedient thing to do at the time.

"The three of us agreed that I would be the spokesman for our group, but at the conclusion of the formal remarks this morning, we will all be willing to take a few questions. I would now like to turn this back to Oscar who has a few more remarks to make. Oscar?"

Oscar Ramirez scanned the audience for a moment or two before he began. "Once I received this information, I immediately called the Attorney General in Washington and let him know what had happened. He was obviously quite disturbed and agreed with the plans that we had immediately set in motion. But I think at this point it is only fitting that I let the Attorney General of the United States, the Honorable Aaron Freedman pick up the story."

With this cue, Aaron Freedman emerged from the sixth limousine and quickly made his way to the microphones. The audience, spectators and press alike, were stunned by this turn of events. No one had even the slightest inkling that the Attorney General of the United States was going to make an appearance at this event.

Aaron Freedman began "Good morning everyone! I am here because of the obviously serious charges which have been made. At this point they are all charges, and a great deal of work remains to be done to confirm everything that has been alleged to have happened over the last few days. However, without going into too much greater detail, we are in possession of at least three tapes which hold the phone calls which were allegedly made. With that evidence in hand we have already set in motion a plan to convene the Federal Grand Jury here in San Antonio. We will be presenting the evidence we have gathered so far, and any other evidence that may yet be turned up in our investigation. We will be seeking indictments, unspecified, of the people involved in this criminal conspiracy and will pursue any and all legal remedies to the fullest extent that Federal Law allows. Neither I nor any of my associates here will comment on what action might be taken by representatives from the State of Texas.

"Furthermore, we have made arrangements, in conjunction with the State Police of Texas and the State Department of Elections to have all ballots placed in protective custody, until plans can be worked out for the eventual recount of all the absentee ballots in the state as a first step toward assuring a fair vote for this state.

"I spoke with the President just before leaving to fly down here and he wanted me to assure everyone that this Administration would not sit still for a single minute in the face of such blatant illegal activity."

The reporters were so busy scribbling notes on their yellow legal pads that they hardly took notice that the Attorney General was obviously not done yet. When he began speaking again their heads all jerked up as if they were on the bottom end of a puppeteer's string.

"These activities were orchestrated by the candidate for President on the Republican ticket. But, they were aimed specifically at the Candidate for President representing the Independence Party. Obviously, it could be construed that we, the incumbent Democratic Administration, are aiming to take out a very strong opponent in this election. To all of you standing here in front of me, and to all Americans, of every political persuasion, listening all around this country and the world at large, I want to assure you that that is definitely *not* the case.

"Indeed, while I was talking to the President about the circumstances surrounding the Governor and all of these Mayors here in Texas, I had occasion to ask him about a rumor that I had heard concerning certain conversations that he, the President, may have had the morning after the election with certain very important people on his election team. This conversation had to do with the uncounted absentee ballots in Illinois in general, and Chicago in particular. It has been alleged that the President may have sought to put pressure on the Mayor of Chicago to make sure that the President ended up securing most of those absentee ballot votes, thus assuring his victory in what has turned out to be a very close race in Illinois."

Aaron stopped and let this sink in for a few seconds. A stunned silence had taken over the couple of thousand people in attendance as they all waited for what most thought was going to be the dropping of the next shoe.

"I want to say to the American people who are listening to this program that I am dreadfully ashamed of what my boss, the President of the United States, said to me over the next several minutes of this conversation which took place in the Oval Office of the White House. He asked me to do whatever would be necessary to "fix" this situation with the Mayor of Chicago and the head of the National Democratic Party. He wanted to know how much, meaning money, it would take to make this thing go away, permanently.

"The President arranged within eight hours to deliver a suitcase to a locker at Dulles Airport that contained ten million dollars in small bills. The key to this suitcase was then delivered to my home.

"Again, just as in the cases down here, there is a tape of the phone conversation made from the White House. Additionally I dispatched an FBI agent to recover the suitcase from Dulles. I also arranged to have another agent posted at my home to witness the turning over of the key to me by the personal secretary to the President of the United States.

"Therefore, as personally painful as it is for me to do, I have also made arrangements to have the Federal Grand Jury for the District of Columbia to convene on Wednesday where

Attorneys from the Justice Department will present all the evidence gathered so far seeking a criminal indictment of the President of the United States for conspiracy to commit an election crime."

There was a flurry of activity in the Press area as reporters ran for their mobile vans, and others sought to get far enough away to be able to use their cell phones to reach their editors all around the country. But Aaron Freedman still was not done.

"I would like to conclude by saying I can hardly convey how deeply disturbed I am personally by all of these events, both in Illinois and here in Texas, and the impact they may possibly have had on this election. At this point in time I really can't say whether ballots were actually tampered with, or whether votes were actually moved from one candidate to another in either Texas or Illinois. I do know that the results announced from both states will be construed as suspicious by a great many people all over the country. The Justice Department with the complete cooperation and assistance of the Federal Bureau of Investigation will stop at nothing to determine what may actually have happened with the ballots.

"Finally, on a personal note, I am deeply saddened and thoroughly ashamed of the behavior of the head of my party, the President of the United States for acting in this manner. I am so ashamed that using this forum this morning, I am now announcing my resignation as Attorney General of the United States. My formal resignation will be delivered to the White House later this afternoon.

"It has been an honor serving my country in this job for the last four years, and I totally enjoyed the challenge it brought. But I cannot for one more minute work in an Administration that would stoop as low as this one did these last few days. So, I thank you all for your support in the past, and for your understanding of why I am doing what I just announced today. Good morning!"

With this, Aaron picked up his brief notes, and made his way back to the last Limousine and was quickly driven away. The two Justice Department attorneys and the Mayors were as dumb-founded as the Press as they stood open to answering some of the zillion questions that came firing at them from all sides.

Chapter 24

At the Willard Hotel in Washington Mark Worthington, Jaime Gonzalez and Gordon Metcalfe and a couple of staffers sat waiting for the talking heads to come on screen. But the network had informed everyone that there would be about a ten minute break before their panel of analysts would review the stunning news of this just completed press conference. Brian Williams simply said, "We all need a little time to digest what we have just heard. We'll be back in a few minutes. Please stay tuned."

Mark turned to Gordon and said, "Gordon, you've been around politics for a long time. Have you *ever* heard anything like this?"

Gordon's reply was quick and to the point. "The only thing that comes close to this was when we finally heard the real depth of the conspiracy in the Nixon white house having to do with Watergate. We were all devastated when we learned the grimy details."

Mark went on "Well, this morning's announcements said that we lost both Texas and Illinois. Those were close races, so it may be legitimate, or maybe we got hosed. What do you all think? Did we get screwed out of one or both of those? 400 votes in Illinois? That sure is damned close. So what do you guys think we should do?"

Paul Matthews, Mark's chief of staff offered "I think we should do whatever we have to do to push for a recount in both states. First of all because of the closeness of the final result in Illinois along with the history of vote tampering that has hung over

Chicago and Cook County for decades. Then secondly, because we know now that at least four of the mayors in Texas rejected Houston completely, but at least one or two, particularly the Mayor of Dallas, did not join them in the protest. That suggests that they *may* have done something to carry out the Governor's demands."

Gordon added "In any case, the results in both states are so close, I think it would be prudent for us to do as Paul suggests. I'll make the necessary calls and add our weight to the demands for a total recount."

Mark got up and walked to the window and slowly turning around said to all of them "Would you ever have believed something like this could have happened in our country? I'll tell you what. I've witnessed a lot of brave acts in my time in the military, but what those three mayors and our Attorney General did today is right up there with the best of them. Paul, I would like to meet with Aaron Freedman as soon as the dust settles a bit. I don't want to compromise the investigation in any way, but I do want to tell him how proud I was when he announced his resignation. I hope we can find a suitable place for him in the new administration, of course assuming that we can win this thing after all.

"But for now, outside of pushing to get those votes recounted, I don't want us to join in the attacks on either Bobby or the President. I don't think we need to pile on either of them – they have enough problems without us joining in. Anyhow, a lot of people from both of the parties will think we are just looking for a way to nail down the Presidency. And honest to God, guys, I don't want to be President so badly that I would think of attacking them at this point. I'm not sure whether it's public opinion or their consciences that will be the hardest for them to deal with! I sure wouldn't want to be in their shoes."

****

At the White House, the small group assembled with the President in the Oval Office listening to the News Conference sat stunned as they waited for the commentators to locate their vocal chords.

The President was the first to comment as he growled "That worthless, ungrateful son of a bitch! Why didn't he quit when he was sitting right here in this office – what was it? Two or three days ago? Miserable bastard. Wonder who got to him? He set me up with that suitcase idea of his."

Martin Remington, the President's personal legal counselor was the next to speak. "I am most uncomfortable with all of this. Sir, did you or did you not make the phone call to Backstrom? Did you or did you not ask Freedman how much it would take? Did you or did you not send *your* secretary to Dulles with the suitcase, and then tell her to drop the key off at Freedman's house?

"You want to know who got to Freedman? I'll tell you who got to him – his conscience got to him! His sense of justice and what is right and what is wrong! Did he also not tell you that he was 'no John Mitchell'?"

The Chief of Staff interrupted with "Who in the hell's lawyer are you Remington? You sound like you are cross examining the President. Aren't you supposed to be defending him and

118

recommending how he can avoid any problems with this thing?"

Remington threw his head back and laughed. "Why you arrogant little prick! Are you so afraid of losing your job that you are going to get all incensed about my asking what are the obvious questions of this man? You think those questions are harsh? Wait till they get his ass on the witness stand. The questions I asked will sound like an invitation to an afternoon tea party."

Remington then turned back to the President. "You, sir, are in one deep pile of shit! I think we had better discuss just what your options are before you get sucked into that Grand Jury. First of all you can deny everything and claim it is all a conspiracy to deny you the Presidency. But, I'll tell you what. That line will sink faster than the Titanic. They have evidence and a lot of it, and they will kill you if you try to pretend it never happened.

"Your second option would be to ride it out for the next eight weeks and just pretend you are too busy to be doing Grand Juries and diversions such as that, and maybe you can make it to January 20th when the new President, whomever he might be, takes over.

"Or, you could just submit your resignation right now and hotfoot it out of town as fast as you can go. I would suspect there are Congressmen right now who are preparing the appropriate orders of impeachment papers, and when all of this sinks in there may not be one or two parties after your scalp, but all three will be vying to get in on the party.

"After what I've heard today, I feel like stopping on my way home and have my suit cleaned. I just feel dirty knowing what you have led us into!

"I will tell you right now – neither my firm nor I want any part of this. I will have a list drawn up of extremely capable defense attorneys around the country that you can look over and decide who you want to defend you from now on. But you will have my resignation perhaps as early as this afternoon. I want no more part of you, this office or this administration."

The President looked up from his desk as Martin Remington picked up his brief case and started for the door. His parting words were "I'm sorry, Martin. I'm truly sorry!"

****

Ellen Livingston and Bob Madison had returned from the Jersey Shore mid afternoon on Sunday and agreed that they would meet in his office on Monday to watch the Texas news conference. Bob also invited the other ten members of their rogue group of Senators and five of them were actually in town and agreed to meet.

They all sat watching what was going on with only an occasional expletive being dropped, or a few 'oh, my Gods' uttered. While they waited for the talking heads to speak, Bob said "I must admit I have never much cared for the President and I actually have a visceral dislike of Bobby Houston, but never in my wildest dreams would I have imagined that either of them could stoop this low!"

Ellen added "I think we better hope that Mark Worthington wins this thing somehow, or we are going to have one hell of a Constitutional crisis if either one of these other slime-bags actually gets chosen to be President."

The consensus was that the country was damn lucky to have someone in the wings with the basic common decency and high level of integrity that Mark Worthington possessed.

****

Senator Jeff Corcoran sat very still when the program from San Antonio faded off the screen. He turned to his chief of staff and almost reverently said "I think, maybe, we should say a little prayer right now. I sure hope that our country will be able to digest this mess and move on with some degree of confidence in all of us here in Washington. God knows, there have to be a whole lot of ordinary people out there who must think that we are all a bunch of crooks – and frankly I wouldn't blame them a bit if that were the conclusion they came to."

He turned to his Chief of Staff and said "Get in touch with Mark Worthington's office at the Willard, and see when I can get in to see him. As soon as possible, if at all possible."

****

Finally, about twenty minutes after the Attorney General left the microphones and the Mayors and local Justice Department Attorneys had finished answering questions, Brian Williams came back on the air and quickly turned the program over to the four commentators.

Richard opened the discussion. "In England I believe they might call this a 'sticky wicket'. Here we have the leading vote getter without quite enough electoral votes to win the election outright. We have the President who might conceivably get enough votes in the House of Representatives to actually win the election, and his very own Attorney General has just filed papers to seek an indictment against the President for what may constitute a felony. AND he is also resigning in protest over the whole bloody mess. Then we have the candidate with the second most popular and electoral votes now accused of ordering the tampering with enough votes to swing the Texas vote to him. The resigning U.S. Attorney General is also convening a Federal Grand Jury seeking conspiracy indictments against him as well!"

Ernie Hardesty was obviously pleased in a way, because it certainly shined a clean bright light on his candidate, Mark Worthington. But Ernie simply said "It's a sad day for all of America. It's like telling 79 or 80 million voters that they have voted for someone who is not morally worthy of being President. What a disappointment!"

Henry had been a long time Republican analyst and he was as stunned as his Democratic counterpart. "I simply don't know what to say. To call this unprecedented is totally inadequate. I guess we all need to wait now and see what the three candidates have to say. We know where the President is, and we know where Mark Worthington is, but have we any idea where Bobby Houston is?"

Peter thought that he better pick up on that question. "I'm quite sure that the President will have a few choice words in the next few hours concerning this whole situation. I have to remind all of you that so far there is nothing but a bunch of allegations out there. Even the so called tapes which they say they have are all just allegations since no one has heard them or knows exactly what they are supposed to contain, or if in fact whether they even exist! So let's not convict these two honorable gentlemen of 'high crimes and misdemeanors' on the basis of what is just hearsay at this moment. Remember, they are both innocent until proven guilty."

Chapter 25

The next morning, after the surprise announcement from Aaron Freedman that he was resigning his post as Attorney General of the United States, the President, his Press Secretary, top domestic policy advisors and new Legal Counsel gathered in the Oval Office.

The President began the meeting by introducing John Sylvester Marshall as his new Attorney General. All of the staff present congratulated Marshall regarding his new position. Marshall was a senior partner at one of the oldest and most prestigious law firms in Philadelphia and had spent many years dealing with a variety of issues at the Capitol. He had advised the President on a few small personal issues earlier in his career. He was of average height, with a nearly full head of snow white hair. At sixty-three he had spent 40 years practicing law and was touted as someone who could make sense out of very complex and difficult issues. His work as a litigator before the Supreme Court was highly regarded and routinely praised by his peers. He was also known to be very tough, bordering on ruthless. He was not a warm and fuzzy person and had very few friends, either male or female. His personal history was marked by four failed marriages.

The President appeared to be more relaxed than he had been in several days and he began the discussion by saying "Well, it looks like we have a bit of a problem to deal with today. John and I spent some time on the phone last night and he thinks he has a way to head off this Congressional investigation that is being talked about. John?"

"I would only disagree with the President over the term 'a bit'. We have one helluva problem gentlemen. However, from what the President tells me, Freedman was the one who suggested that it would cost a lot of money to 'fix' the Illinois outcome. It was Freedman who came up with the five to ten million dollar figure, and the President tells me that it was Freedman who suggested using the secretary to move the money to Dulles. Is that the understanding of all of you?"

The group that was listening to this nodded their agreement, because all they knew was what the President had told them, since none of them had been present during the discussion about the money.

Marshall went on "The President also told me that Freedman said that he knew where he could get his hands on that kind of money, and he was the one who stuffed the suitcase with the bills. The story as I understand it was that Freedman met the President's secretary in the parking lot of the Jefferson Memorial and gave her the suitcase with instructions to deliver the key to him that night. She did what she was instructed to do and although she is temporarily out of the office, I'm sure we can count on her willingness to swear under oath that this was how it happened. Simply speaking it was Mr. Freedman who is the culprit here and as the newly appointed Attorney General I will go to the Federal Grand Jury for the District of Columbia tomorrow seeking an indictment of Mr. Freedman on grounds of criminal behavior."

The chief political advisor asked "What about the phone call tape?"

Marshall replied that he thought "The President could quash that kind of evidence on the grounds that any phone call that was taped without judicial approval would constitute another illegal activity and therefore Freedman has no case. Anyhow, as the new AG I will be directing the Grand Jury to forget the case brought by the old Attorney General. By the time this all plays out we will be well through the recount of the disputed votes, the counting of the electoral ballots and we'll be close to the voting in the House of Representatives. We think the President has a solid chance of winning the election based on the makeup of the House, since he only needs 26 state caucuses to elect him. So it looks to me like the whole affair should be over by the January 20th inauguration date. The President will either be returned to office in which case we can then make a determination that we have insufficient evidence to pursue Freedman and the whole case will be dropped – and likely forgotten forever! Or if the President loses, he can leave office with his head held high."

The new political advisor came back one more time with "The only problem I see is if Congress decides to bring impeachment charges against the President, based on Freedman's story. What do you think of that possibility?"

Marshall responded "The Congress will be so involved with all the issues having to do with the recounting of ballots in Texas and Illinois plus having to deal with the electoral vote count that they simply won't have the time or the backbone to set up the impeachment process, even if one or two of the real Hawks in the Republican Party think it is the right thing to do. And anyhow, those guys don't have a lot of standing with the mainstream party so they'll be easy to ignore. There is so much on everyone's mind right now that I just don't see any groundswell to bring charges against the President, especially since he may be leaving office in less than two months anyhow.

What we need to do is concentrate on lowering the temperature regarding the President's involvement with the voting thing, and work like hell getting the House to vote him back into office!"

With that said the meeting broke up with several very quiet people leaving the oval office wondering about the path their boss was about to lead them down.

****

The President's Press Secretary notified the networks that the President was prepared to make a statement concerning the circumstances surrounding the resignation of the Attorney General at 5:00pm EST. The broadcast would be from the Oval Office and there would be no reporters present, and therefore no question and answer period.

At the appointed hour The President introduced John Sylvester Marshall as the new acting Attorney General. After a few glowing comments about the broad experience and highly regarded reputation for integrity possessed by the new Attorney General, the President then proceeded to detail his plan of action.

"Good evening everyone. It has been a long and difficult week since the election. As everyone knows there have been allegations floating around concerning the ballot results in both Texas and in Illinois.

"You also are aware of the sudden and unexpected resignation of Aaron Freedman, the Attorney General of the United States. I have received and accepted his letter. And now as I have already mentioned I have prevailed upon John Sylvester Marshall, a long time friend of this office and participant in Washington affairs for over 30 years, to step in as Acting Attorney General pending ratification by the Senate.

"Today we have also set in motion several initiatives.

    a. We will continue to investigate the allegations concerning potential voting irregularities in Texas, and we will be seeking indictments of several persons by the Federal Grand Jury in San Antonio.

    b. After careful consideration of the facts I have authorized Attorney General Marshall to pursue an indictment of former Attorney General Aaron Freedman for his role in the events surrounding the possible ballot tampering in Illinois. This investigation will also deal with the false and malicious accusations which Mr. Freedman leveled at this office which were obviously intended to spread a heavy smokescreen over his own role in this affair.

    c. In light of the information just uncovered the request to the District of Columbia Grand Jury initiated by Aaron Freedman which wrongly and maliciously implicated the Oval Office in the 'Illinois affair' has been withdrawn.

"The chairman of the Republican National Committee has suggested that I should resign my office in light of all these allegations. I want to reiterate to you the American people that there is absolutely no merit to these malicious charges made by

Aaron Freedman and for that reason alone I will not consider for even a minute the possibility of resigning from this office.

"As developments unfold we will, as always, be back before you to keep you informed.

"Good evening and may God Bless America!"

****

The television network that Jack and Roger worked for barely had enough advance notice to even get these two stalwarts in studio to comment on the President's brief message. As for the other experts they usually called in, that would have to wait for another day.

Jack opened the few minutes that had been made available for analysis with "Roger, I am frankly stunned by this telecast. Aaron Freedman as Attorney General just a day or so earlier had implicated the President in some kind of conspiracy to perhaps steal enough votes to carry the election in the State of Illinois. He certainly sounded very sure of himself as he laid out the course of action that the Justice Department was going to take with regard to both Governor Houston and the President. In fact he was so certain he had directed his attorneys in both Texas and the District of Columbia to pursue indictments by Federal Grand Juries. And then to emphasize just how disgusted he was with the whole sordid situation he submitted his resignation to the President! Now this……this…what do we call it? This knee jerk reaction from the Oval Office? I am just stunned!"

Roger answered "I certainly hear you. Nearly everyone I talked to figured that the President's options were to: a) resign and just fade out of the picture; b) or hang on for the next few weeks until after the electoral votes are cast, and the Senate gets the ballots to count. The best possible case would have him winning the vote outright, or be in a solid position to get the House delegations to vote for him over the other two. At that point he could rightly begin his defense of all these charges. But no one I know ever thought for a minute that he would nullify the charges against himself, and initiate an attack on Freedman. It's simply unbelievable!"

"Do you think he can get away with this? Is there any merit in his version of the story? And what about the Secretary? Is she going to be forced to lie about her role in all of this? And by the way just where is she right now? She is a long time loyal Democrat and loyal Presidential aide, but will she be willing to possibly perjure herself to save this President? Does the new Attorney General think that he is clever enough to make this happen?"

"Yeah, and what happens if the Senate calls confirmation hearings real quick and rejects him? There sure are a lot of unanswered questions and very sticky constitutional issues surrounding this whole mess."

Jack then closed the brief follow up analysis with this observation. "Roger, I can't help but reflect on what this feels like. This has all the same vibes that we were all getting about Richard Nixon and the way he handled the Watergate mess. There were lies all around and the more the President and the men around him lied, the worse the situation got. Then finally he had to resign in disgrace, just before Congress was about to kick him out through the impeachment process. Most of his closest advisors ended up going to prison and this scene tonight smells an awful lot like that cesspool did!"

Chapter 26

Mark Worthington had left his Chicago hotel moving on to Washington where he took a suite of rooms at the historic old Willard Hotel. He had asked a small group of advisors including Jaime Gonzalez and Gordon Metcalfe to meet at the Hotel about 10:30 so they could all talk after this mysterious news conference in Texas was concluded. They were all anticipating a spate of announcements during the morning which might shape the course of national politics for several years to come

But additionally all of this news was going to impact them heavily in one way or another. Either Mark Worthington was going to become President, or he was going back to Illinois to resume his University teaching duties. Jamie Gonzalez was either going to wield the gavel in the Senate as the next Vice President and President of the Senate, or he was going to be sitting somewhere on the floor as the Junior Senator from Florida, and member of the minority Independence Party.

Perhaps the only one who probably wasn't going to be touched in a big time personal way was Gordon Metcalfe, who had already let Mark know that he wanted to retire back to California, giving up his job as Chairman of the Independence Party. Mark had heard him out and simply demurred. Mark was not at all sure that he could afford to let Gordon slip away that easily.

****

Mark and his group sat in a circle since Mark carried none of the ego baggage that so many politicians were burdened with. He clearly knew that this group of people in particular were responsible for him being in the position he was at this very moment. Without their support and advice and very hard work he would certainly be back in Champaign grading papers.

Mark started the discussion by directing a question to Jeff Corcoran, Senator from Ohio and an ardent supporter from the very beginning. "Jeff, I have two questions that I would like your input on. First how do you view our chances in the House if this thing does indeed go that far? And secondly, if we do win this thing, how do you see the Senate shaping up, now that there will clearly be three political parties dividing up those nice little desks down there on the Senate floor?"

Everyone including Jeff chuckled at this reference to the "nice little desks", but Jeff responded "I'd like to answer the 2nd question first if I might. It is going to be historic if for no other reason than we will have to actually create three sections, left, center and right. I would think that we, the Independence Party will probably end up in the middle which is where we are ideologically anyhow. Right now it looks to me like we have 8 clear cut winners who have taken up the Independence banner, but all the scuttlebutt I have been hearing – and it is a lot of chatter – I think it is entirely possible that as many as 4 Democrats and 7 Republicans who didn't have to run for election this year may well change their registration and come with us. You honestly hit a lot of really sensitive nerves with a lot of those people who have always been considered moderates in their own party and now they see a real comfortable way to disassociate themselves from the real diehards on both sides of the aisle, and stand as a true Independent. As I say this whole exercise is going to be *truly* historic.

"Also, if I am right, and we come up with as many as 15 or 20 Senators in our caucus, we can effectively force both sides to address issues from a moderate, what's good for the country position. Neither of them would ever be able to get 51 votes for any legislation without us, so that means we can really have a positive impact on legislation. I'm really excited about that possibility, because I am so damned tired of all the crap that has been going on for far too long. Neither one of the extremes wants to give an inch and now we will force them into being more statesmanlike, if you will."

Mark replied, "That sounds really hopeful, not just for us, but for the country as a whole. I can't help but think that that is exactly why we got so much support – the voters want an end to all this radical left, radical right stuff and a return to some degree of sanity. What about our chances in the House?"

"Yeah, I knew you were going to bring me back to that. I wish I was as positive on that one as I am on the Senate organization. I'm sure that Gordon, Joe and Cody have more insight into what it looks like in the House than I do, so I'd like to hear from one of them. Guys?"

Cody, who keeps track of all the numbers and who was sitting in a side chair spoke up. "Sure, Senator. Right now the Democrats control the House and 26 of the 50 delegations, the Republicans control 21 and 3 of the delegations are evenly split. So just based on that configuration here's the bad news. If those 26 states vote for the President then he's our new President. But that isn't taking into consideration any of the unprecedented – if you will pardon my French - shit that has happened in the last few days. So here is what we do know and then what we suspect may happen.

"First of all, there were at least 70 Representatives elected under our Independence Party designation: 43 were newly elected candidates to Congress, but 27 were incumbents who defected from the other parties. 20 of those were Republicans and 7 Democrats. The way I have it figured those 27 men and women are going to play a huge part in how those states vote. Under the old way of doing things the Representatives would only have had 2 choices: vote for the Republican challenger, or the incumbent President. But look at what those people have to consider now: first, a highly likeable and very qualified Independent who carried more than 44% of the popular vote – far more than either of the other two candidates. Secondly, the Republican candidate, Gov. Houston has been humiliated and is now under indictment for voter fraud. Third, the President trailed both of the other two and then he has humiliated himself by directing an effort to tamper with ballots in Illinois and may end up being indicted himself. Although that may not happen it remains to be seen what will actually happen to him.

"All that said it certainly wouldn't be much of a stretch for a whole lot of those folks to vote for the only unsullied and very much most popular candidate – our very own Mark"

"Thank you Cody. I guess that means that we will just have to trust that enough of these folks will find it so distasteful to vote for their candidate that they will turn to us. What do you think Gordon?"

Gordon Metcalfe, a veteran of political party politics for over 40 years paused for an abnormally long period of time before answering Mark. "I've played the game of politics for a very long time – longer than I really care to admit – and political alliances, and loyalties run very deep in nearly all of these folks. On the surface, considering all the points that Cody so eloquently related just a minute ago, I would say we would be runaway winners. But, unfortunately, political roots run very, very deep. The sponsors, the organizations, the money trees, the years of being in power – all of these things are right up front in the minds of these politicians. For the most part, they are not Statesmen. Mind you, they are not all party hacks either. But very few of them are truly statesmen. So for them to abandon the party they have been a part of for 10, 20, 30, 40, 50 years – that will take a great leap of statesmanlike behavior for several hundred politicians. Can that happen? Yes, it can happen. But, will it happen? I just don't know. I really don't know. But, my gut tells me, it's not likely!"

****

Mark then directed his attention to the group as a whole. "We have talked about so many issues over the last several months, I would like each of you to pick 4 issues that you feel so strongly about that you think they should be singled out in the first few days of our new administration. I will do the same. But I want you to give me a brief on each of those. Now I do mean brief. I don't want a 100 page footnoted document. 2, 3 or 4 pages that clearly tell me why we should expend the political capital we have available in those few days on your favorite projects. Then we'll consider all of them along with mine and get ready in the next 15 or 20 days to lay out just what we want to do. Everyone okay with that?"

All the people in the room nodded okay and quickly disbursed to get to work on their new project, although as it turned out lately, all of them had already done work on numerous ideas they wanted the new administration to address, but now it would come down to minimalizing their output and establishing some priorities.

Chapter 27

The reaction from around the country was swift and to some little extent followed predictable party lines. The die-hards on the Democratic left applauded the President for his fighting back and generally had nothing good to say about Aaron Freedman. The conservative right wing of the Republicans decried the continuing witch hunt against their man – Bobby Houston, but at the same time they clearly thought he was guiltier than sin, and was merely trying to divert attention from his own problems. But, now that someone with solid middle of the road credentials seemed to be on the verge of getting elected President, there was a huge group of people in the middle, some Republicans, some Democrats and nearly all of those who dared to declare themselves as Independence Party independents, declared a plague on both of their houses. They simply believed both the President *and* the Governor to be guilty as charged.

* * * * * * * * * * * * * *

In Iowa Charlie Wipperman and his wife were enjoying dinner with the Governor, Earl Potts, and his wife, and former Senator Ernie Hardesty and his wife at the Hardesty's home. Of course the topic of discussion over cocktails was dominated by the President's announcement.

Earl shook his head in disbelief as he tried to process what had just happened. "I guess about the only way you can look at it is he believes the best defense is an outrageous offense!"

Ernie took a sip of his martini and offered "I think he is simply buying time. His own Attorney General had already fired the silver bullet into his head, and he just wants to throw up enough road blocks and smoke screens to get him to the opening of the electoral votes – and probably until January 20th. The Congress is going to be really busy, with all of the uncertainty about how the Government is going to be organized……"

At this point Charlie Wipperman's wife asked what he meant by the uncertainty about organizing the government.

"Well, you know, with three real political parties in Congress trying to decide who will be Speaker of the House, and Senate majority leader when no one has a real majority……stuff like that. Who has time to worry about organizing an impeachment effort?"

Earl summed it all up by saying "I think you are right Ernie. But I will tell you this: his dirty fingers are all over that suitcase full of money, and there will be at least one – if not more – congressional committees wanting to get to the bottom of that mess – like just where did the money come from? I can't believe his secretary would actually lie to protect him but I suppose stranger things have happened in Washington politics."

Charlie then murmured "That is unless she has already been stuffed in her own suitcase somewhere up river."

****

November in Arizona reminds everyone why they came, and stayed, in Arizona in the first place. Little or no humidity and temperatures in the low 80's! Just a little slice of 'Heaven on Earth'. Bryce Randolph was enjoying every moment of the evening sitting with Jaclyn on the patio before dinner enjoying a glass of his favorite Chimney Rock Cabernet. Finally their conversation got around to politics and she asked what he thought about the President's attack on Aaron Freedman.

"Well, you know there have always been a lot of strange things going on in Washington, but it sure seems to me that this is really one of the strangest. I think everyone was totally shocked when the Attorney General - the President's *own* Attorney General – wrapped up that little soiree in San Antonio with the accusations about the President doing the same thing only in Illinois! That just has to tell you something, doesn't it? His own Attorney General accusing him of what is surely a crime? But then just when he could have stepped back and washed his hands of the whole mess –he resigns, which sort of just puts an exclamation point on what he just told the country."

Jaclyn responded "You know dear, I am so happy you are back here and our lives are starting to return to normal. I missed you when you were gone all those months – and even though you were working with a lot of nice people, there are just so many nut cases involved in politics that I was afraid that something might happen to you!"

Then smiling Bryce replied "Well, I made it without a scratch, but now I'm really afraid for the country. The guy who just got through making that announcement is the same guy who has his finger on the ultimate weapons in this country. He controls the FBI and the Military and the Secret Service and the CIA! Now he turns around and goes like a mad dog after one of his own men. That really scares me, because who else might he go after in the few weeks he has left in office? Honestly, I'm beginning to wonder if he hasn't suffered some kind of aneurism or something. That announcement he just made sounded like a crazy thing for him to do. So, yes, I'm really glad to be home too!"

****

Ellen Livingston was in a meeting with Bob Madison and several of the other Senators so affectionately known as the Maverick Twelve, when they broke to listen to the President's news broadcast. Bob made the first comment "Please pinch me and tell me I didn't hear what I think I just heard."

He turned to one of the others who had been a very successful physician before entering politics and he asked "Do you think he has had a breakdown or something? How did that sound to you?"

The Doctor who represented Oklahoma in the Senate suggested "It really sounds to me like he is so desperate to stay in his job, that he is willing to act like a crazy-man to avoid going before a Grand Jury. Actually I haven't been around him for several months, so I can't say that I have noticed any particular change in his recent behavior."

Ellen Livingston then suggested that his decision to get rid of all of those people who were appointed by his late predecessor may have been an indication that something wasn't right with his thinking. "I do know that he is reported to have exploded at some of his staff when they referred to him as the 'accidental President'. You know, after all, it isn't like he was elected to the job! He *is* an accidental President! So live with it!"

One of the others in the group then summed it up by saying "He's just not the kind of guy to slough off something like that.

141

He is super sensitive to the fact that he was never able to get the American public excited about all his runs for the nomination, and so I can just imagine he is probably super-sensitive to any kind of criticism. And man, oh, man, didn't his Attorney General really hand him the ultimate in put downs! Yeah, I think he may have had some kind of incident that we haven't been told about – or maybe even his Doctors aren't aware of."

Chapter 28

Aaron Freedman had returned to Washington immediately after the press conference in San Antonio and had holed up in his house with his wife. There were press vehicles parked on the street across from the house, but neither he nor his wife had ventured out, or given any kind of statement whatsoever.

Aaron's wife Pamela peeked out the front room window and half turning said "Do you suppose they sleep in that van? Hoping that one or both of us will go out for milk or something?"

Aaron said "Well, I don't know about the sleeping part, but you can be sure that there will be someone awake in the front seat every minute until we do make an appearance. You'll notice that there are at least three other news vans out there as well as the NBC one right across the street. That must make our neighbors real happy, but I guess that is what you can expect when you allow a political animal on your street. Fits pretty neatly with the old saying "there goes the neighborhood!"

"Oh, come on now. The people on this street think you're a really special guy and they are going to be completely understanding of what is going on."

"That may be, but I think I will feel better after Peter gets here and we have a chance to sort this whole thing out. Peter is not only a good friend but he is a first rate defense attorney, and who knows what I may be needing as this fiasco unfolds. My tendency is to go out there and make some kind of statement, but Pete may have a different idea about doing that. Waiting an additional three or four hours to figure out what I should do or say won't hurt anything."

"Aaron, What do you think about what the President just said? He's trying to make you the villain. Can he make any of that crap stick on you?"

"I don't think so. I really think he is a day late and a dollar short on this one. Of course he can pull the Grand Jury requests back as far as the Governor and the Mayor are concerned. I'm sure that his new AG had to agree to refuse to pursue anything as far as the White House is concerned.

"You know Pam, the funny thing about this is the position the President is in right now. He has about two months until the next inauguration. In that few weeks he could actually be declared the winner of the election, depending on whether no one gets enough electoral votes to win outright – and right now Mark Worthington does not have enough. So, it is theoretically possible that the House of Representatives voting as 50 states could possibly pick him to be President ……"

"You don't really think that could happen, now do you?"

"No, I don't, but as I said, in theory it could happen. What is more likely is the House would do the honorable thing and select the candidate that got the most popular votes and the most electoral votes – and that would be Mark Worthington. But you have the Representatives from 50 states involved and you have three candidates and three parties – God, it really gets complicated!"

"Well, whatever. I just don't want him coming after you. I am so proud of you I just can't tell you how much I admire what you did – and you sure don't deserve some kind of witch hunt chasing after you for no more reason than getting some revenge!"

"No, I don't either. But politics being what they are, it wouldn't surprise me if he doesn't try to destroy me in some way or another. By the way did I tell you that I got a phone call from someone on Mark Worthington's transition team wanting to set up a face to face meeting for me with Worthington in a day or so. He wanted to know if I could make the time available."

"And....?"

"I said I would love to meet with the General but since I no longer have an office or a Secretary, just call me at home and we'll work out the details."

"You don't suppose......"

"Pam, I don't suppose anything. Let's just see how things work out."

****

Bobby Houston was sitting with his wife watching the President speak on Television about the impending investigations. She turned to him and said "I haven't gotten overly involved with your political twists and turns Bobby. I always trusted that you would do the right thing when big decisions were going to be made. But, this whole thing just doesn't smell right to me. Did you really try to influence the election? I think I have a right to know, because it is going to affect our whole family whether you did or not. But, I guess it could be really bad if you did what they are saying you did. The kids, your Mom and Dad, the rest of the family......you know what I mean?"

Bobby turned to her with two big tears starting to trickle down his cheek. He swallowed hard and with a voice that was barely audible he answered her question. "I was so angry when I saw how close we got to winning it all – I just lost it. I was so angry. I just couldn't believe that goddamn General was going to take it all away from me! I just couldn't believe it. I'd worked so hard – for so long – and just like that he comes riding in on his big white horse and takes it away from me. I just couldn't believe it.

"It wouldn't be so bad if they didn't have the tapes. But I know they do. The funny thing is we didn't really mess with any tapes – as far as I know none of the Mayors did a damn thing. They all pretended like they were trying to do something but none of them did anything! So nothing was done. And it looks like we won Texas anyway. All of this didn't have to be if I had just kept my damn big mouth shut!"

"Can they convict you of a crime for what you said? Considering that nothing actually happened?"

"I don't really know if they can. The problem is they can make it sound so bad, that I'll be ruined whether they have any kind of case or not."

"So what are you going to do? Are you going to resign? What's going to happen to us? Did you ever think of us Bobby?" She turned away trying to keep from sobbing. "Did you ever think of us?"

Bobby sat with his head down and the tears rolling down his face onto his shirt. He couldn't bear to look at her and he couldn't answer her, because he knew the answer to the question. He never thought of anyone but himself – ever. So there it was. He of the big ego, never thought of anyone else, and now he was about to be humbled beyond his wildest comprehension. He didn't know what he was going to do – simple as that. He didn't know.

✶✶✶✶✶✶✶✶✶✶✶✶✶✶✶✶✶✶✶✶✶

The highlight of the six o'clock news that night was a just released Gallup poll that found the President's popularity was down to just under 15%. The same poll questions about Bobby Houston found that only about 12% of those polled found Bobby Houston's performance acceptable.

On the other hand the polls found that voting age people in the country thought Mark Worthington's performance through this entire campaign was rated in the low 90% level.

In a companion poll 94% of those questioned thought Mark Worthington should be President while the other two candidates barely registered on the meter.

Chapter 29

Cyndy Black had promised her husband, writer John Black, that she would try to get in touch with Cissy Gonzalez at some time after the heat of the election had simmered down a bit. She tried a couple of different locations before she finally hit on the idea of calling Lucy Fowler who was a younger sorority sister of both Cyndy and Cissy at Northwestern. She knew that Lucy had gotten married to Chad Denson who had been a big time staffer with some Senator, so she figured Lucy would know how to get in touch with Cissy.

When Lucy picked up the phone and heard that it was Cyndy calling she was absolutely thrilled. "Cyndy, I haven't heard from you in a month of Sundays. How are you? And where are you? I didn't recognize the area code. So tell me all about yourself."

Cyndy couldn't help but start laughing as she considered all the questions that Lucy had just fired away at her. "You haven't changed a bit Lucy. Do you pepper your husband with a million questions every night when he comes home from work?"

Lucy said "Oh, no, not really, but I was just so surprised by your call that I guess it all came out at once. Was I always like that?"

"Well, honestly, you were a lot like that but frankly that was what made everybody like you so much. Bubbly, excitable, enthusiastic about everything, and it doesn't sound like you have changed much!"

"Well, thanks Cyndy, that is really nice of you to say that. But do tell me about yourself. What's up with you? And for heavens sake, what ever led you to call me? But there I go again – more questions."

Cyndy laughed and said, well naturally, I needed something and I thought you might just be able to help me. I want to get in touch with Cissy Gordon who I know married the next Vice President. Can you help me?"

"Oh, sure. At least for now Jamie is still the Senator from Florida. But, I've been close to them for some time now. Actually they were at our wedding. But why don't I give you a number that will get you right in to Cissy. So, what are you and your husband up to? As a matter of fact I don't even know what your husband does – isn't he some kind of writer? "

"Yes, he is a writer and that is what I want to talk to Cissy about. John wants to do a book on the 'Making of a President' kind of like those books about Kennedy – remember hearing about them?

"Anyhow, he thought that Cissy and her Senator, soon to be Vice President, would be great inside sources as to how this whole thing came about. What do you think?"

"Sounds exciting, but tell you what – my husband would also be a good contact for you, because he has been a Senator's chief of staff and then a consultant to the Governor of Texas in his run for the Presidency. Unfortunately, he had enough of Bobby Houston's morals quite some time before this latest ballot fiasco. But I can tell you for sure that Chad doesn't think Houston's above doing what they say he did – you know threatening the Mayors and stuff. He's a real nasty guy!"

"Do you think Chad would talk to my guy about all of this?"

"I'm sure he will. I'll tell Chad about what John is up to, and I know he will be happy to talk to him about what he knows. Now don't keep me waiting any longer and tell me what else is going on in your life!"

Chapter 30

Mark Worthington welcomed Gordon Metcalf into his suite with a warm handshake and an offer for coffee, which Gordon happily accepted. "Gordon, we are scheduled to meet in a few days to go over the transition planning and up to now I've been reluctant to name anyone as my Chief of Staff. As you certainly know I don't have the depth of political contacts that you and many of the other people on the team have. So, I've sort of acted as my own Chief. But, it's time, probably past time, when I need to make that decision. I would like you to take that job. How about it?"

To say that Gordon was stunned would be putting it mildly. Never at a loss for words, he sat unusually quiet for a few minutes. The President-elect simply sipped on his coffee and waited. Finally Gordon responded, "I have to tell you that I never expected this. I have been happy – really more than happy – to be a part of this team as we get you ready for the Presidency. But, ever since my wife passed away I've also been looking forward to the peace and quiet of just slipping away into a life kind of like Bryce Randolph has down there in Arizona. A little golf, a lot of reading, some writing, some time with my kids and grand kids. I'm 62 years old now, and, and……"

Mark set his coffee cup down and smiling said, "my oh my, that does sound good doesn't it, especially at such an advanced age! But, Gordon, is that really what you want? I need someone with your experience, your time in the game, and especially someone I totally respect and trust. I need you!

"Let me tell you how I see us running this office. I have a great deal of faith in Jaime and I think he will make a great Vice President and someday President. I want to set us up as a team. You, Jamie and me. We will meet nearly every day, and we will set the agenda. I truly intend to make Jamie a real part of this administration – no pushing him off to the side, to attend funerals and weddings, and stuff like that. I intend that the three of us will confer and hopefully agree on all major appointments, on all policy initiatives and on all long term plans. Your job will be a lot more than just managing the White House staff. You will have real input on everything this administration undertakes in the next four years. Does that make you want to rethink whether you really want to head off to Napa Valley right away?"

Gordon seemed to immediately regain his tongue and he replied "I guess I secretly hoped that you would find some small role in the administration where I could occasionally offer some advice or help to you – but this – this is so much more. I am so totally flattered, and honored that you would think of me filling this role. Yes, of course I will accept your offer. Short of my wife accepting my proposal so many, many years ago, this is far and away the most incredible thing that has ever happened to me! Thank you Mr. President!"

With that Gordon and Mark both stood and shook hands, and Mark said "I'm still Mark to you Gordon, the Mr. President still has a little work to be done before we get to the Mister part. But I am really excited that you want on the team; so let's get over to the Conference room and join the rest of the team. This should be fun because I can now announce the first big appointment of my almost-administration!"

****

Mark opened the daily team meeting with an announcement. "I want all of you to be the first to know that I have offered the position of Chief of Staff to Gordon Metcalfe and he has enthusiastically accepted."

There was an immediate round of applause as everyone stood and began making their way to Gordon to congratulate him on his new position. Mark stood nearby and accepted congratulations from everyone as well on the astuteness of his decision.

Mark continued the meeting by asking Joe Bonafacio how things were progressing on the Elector front. Joe replied "I think we are doing quite well actually. Either I or one of my two assistants has actually talked to over 75 of the electors so far. These are electors who are supposedly committed to either the President or Bobby Houston and who come from states where they are not legally required to vote for the candidate who won that state. None of them were willing to commit to us that they were going to switch their vote to us. But several were definitely interested in hearing how electors have changed their votes in the past, and in finding out more about the fact that they were not legally bound to the person who carried the state. After we finished the calls we sat down and compared our notes and we felt comfortable in reporting that we feel as many as 12 electors might very well switch. That would be more than we need to secure the election."

Paul Matthews, Mark's Press Secretary reported, "As we all agreed, we have refrained from making any comment one way or the other concerning what is going on in Texas and Illinois.

We have not had to make any requests for recounts, because the closeness of the election triggered automatic recounts anyhow. I would like to defer to Senator Corcoran on the impeachment rumors….Senator?”

“First of all, on behalf of all of us on this team, I want to congratulate Gordon and thank you Mark for making such a wise decision. A simply outstanding choice! As you may well guess there is a whole lot of politicking going on up on the Hill. There are so many balls in the air right now it is just a little short of crazy. The last thing on the mind of most Congressmen right now is impeaching the President. I think just about everyone thinks you are going to win Mark, so why bother mucking up the party by pursuing impeachment?

“On the other hand, if the President actually did what is being alleged, then it probably satisfies “high crimes, etc.” and he should be impeached! But, let’s face it. We don’t have months and months to look into all of these charges and follow through on the hearings and then the vote. We have about 5 weeks until they open those elector ballots, and if the outcome is like Joe suggests, then it is simply a moot question. Mark wins, the President leaves office in disgrace in any case, and he joins the Andrew Johnson, James Buchanan, Warren Harding foursome as abject failures as a President. Case closed. I think we should keep our hands out of it. If the Republicans or even some of the Democrats want a pound of flesh from him, so be it. But, I think the Independence Party should stay clear.”

Several comments were made around the table and then Mark said, “I agree, and so Paul, let it be known that we have no position to take on this issue, and that we urge our party members and followers to refrain from getting involved, letting the prosecutors and the courts run their course.”

Chapter 31

It was a bright, sunny day in Washington when Mark Worthington and his inner circle staff came together in a conference room at the Willard and got really serious about organizing their administration. Committees had already been put together a few weeks before to explore possibilities for various cabinet posts, and now the results of those meetings were ready for the group to look at.

Mark was especially interested in knowing who the 'experts' felt should be considered for State, Defense, Treasury and Attorney General. He stated "It's not that I am not interested in the other departments, because I really am, but I think the most work has to be done on these four. So, let's hear what everyone thinks."

So for the next hour or so, the team made up of the almost – elected-President, Jaime Rodriguez, the almost-elected-Vice President – and Gordon Metcalfe, the campaign manager extraordinaire along with three other highly regarded staff members. They quietly and thoughtfully discussed the merits of the various people whose names had been proposed.

No decisions were made but Mark wanted to be sure that a thorough vetting had been done so that there would be no surprises such as moral issues, or resume padding, and whether or not any of these people had even the slightest interest in taking one of the jobs. The staff understood his concern and agreed that they would begin the serious part of the investigation as soon as the meeting was over.

Mark spoke briefly to the group before they broke "You all know that this whole thing is still up for grabs, but I think that we are close enough now that we have to approach our decisions on these people we are looking at as if we did in fact win the election. We have an enormous challenge ahead of us and I guess I don't have to remind you of that. But, if we do come out on top we have to consider that we are more than the outsiders coming in here – we are neither Republicans nor Democrats - we are Independents! We have shaped our message to appeal to the Independent people of this country. We showed sympathy to a number of minorities like the blacks, the gays, women, the Jewish voters and all of those people who are sick and tired of the very special interests that are so deeply rooted in both of the old parties. And, I remind you that we are going into a Congress where we will be the decided minority unless Gordon can pull off some kind of miracle and "convert" a couple hundred more Congressmen to our side.

"I don't think I need to remind you that the people we choose for these key positions still have to be approved by the Senate - so we have to be absolutely certain that we offer up the very brightest and best and squeaky clean candidates possible - an offer 'they can't refuse'!

"We've definitely got our work cut out for us, because we really need the best minds and the most dedicated and sensitive men and women we can possibly identify to help us carry through on our ideas. I am not interested on paying off any particular interests or factions by 'giving' them a cabinet post. I want people who will participate in our cabinet discussions, and who will not be afraid to challenge our ideas. This is not going to be a rubber stamp Cabinet, but rather each one of the members will have a real voice in how this administration approaches their opportunity to run the country. My sense is that this has not been the case for a long time, and it is high time we used these people to help us be successful. Do any of you have any difficulty with this approach – if so, let's hear it right now. No time like the present to start this participative type of government I have in mind."

Mark looked around the room and it was quickly apparent that the "Inner Circle" was in full agreement. Gordon Metcalfe , now officially settled in as the White House Chief of Staff reported that he had set several of his staff to work calling on all of the Electors that had been certified as eligible to vote in December for Mark. It was a little known fact that the electors in only 9 states were legally bound to cast their vote for the candidate that carried their state. Gordon reported "I really don't expect any defections but it will just be prudent to make sure that our folks are all rock solid.

"But additionally we are going to reach out to the electors in a few states including both Texas and Illinois and make some discreet inquiries as to whether any of them might be of a mind to switch their vote to Mark. They are Republicans in Texas and Democrats in Illinois and generally are died in the wool Party partisans – many holding some appointed position or other. But we have to consider the really bad taste in their mouths they must have with regard to the rotten behavior of their candidates. So, it is not out of the realm of possibility that we might be able to come up with the 10 votes we need right there. It is certainly worth a few letters and follow-up phone calls and a few visits. I will be asking our old friend Bryce Randolph to come in and help us get that program underway."

All except Gordon rose quickly and returned to their various rooms to get to work on the selection process.

Gordon moved to a chair next to Mark and said "I couldn't leave without telling you how moved I was with your comments today. We have such an awesome responsibility as well as opportunity – and I didn't want to leave this room without telling you how proud I am to be a part of this. It's history in the making, and as unaccustomed as I am to saying something like this, I'm simply humbled to be here! Thank you!"

****

Mark made his way up to his suite and found his wife and daughter waiting for him. He gave Janet a big hug and then another one for his only daughter, Martha. "I am so glad to see you sweetheart – when did you get here?"

"About an hour ago – everything is so exciting right now, I just couldn't stay at school and not be here for you and Mom." Martha was a 22 year old Senior at Stanford, and she wasn't about to miss all the excitement of the final days of this campaign.

"As your Mother has probably told you already my available personal time is shrinking every day, and if we do pull this thing off your Mother is really going to need your help pretty soon. You know, new house and all."

"I was just telling Mom that I am taking a few months off to be here with you two and do whatever I can to help. This is really exciting Dad. And we didn't have to move to Mumbai or some other god-forsaken place like we've done a few times in our lives!"

"Now, listen here young lady. Don't tell me that you didn't enjoy our stay in Germany? Now did you?"

"Germany was great! But Seoul? No thanks!"

With that Martha gave her Dad a big hug and kiss and whispered in his ear "But a big White house? Yessssss!"

Chapter 32

As a primary candidate for the Presidency Mark Worthington qualified for Secret Service protection for his family and himself. As he was finishing up his breakfast in his suite at the Willard Hotel, he got a very soft buzz on his cell phone. The Secret Service said that they had Aaron Freedman at the elevator on the floor below who said he had an appointment.

Mark responded with a positive, and Janet said "I'll clear out of here. I know you have some important things to talk to him about" and she prepared to leave the room.

Mark took her hand and said, "No, wait a second. I'd like you to meet him - for at least a few minutes. I'm told he is a very engaging person, and I'd like your considered take. Okay?"

Janet agreed, and went into the kitchen to be sure that there was a fresh pot of coffee ready for them.

****

Aaron was quite taken back by the warmth with which he was received by Mark and Janet Worthington. He had heard that Mark was the real thing, and of course he had listened to a lot of the debates and speeches. But what he hadn't expected was the genuineness – and all he could think of was the contrast between this man who was on the verge of becoming the next President of the United States and the little man who was flailing about in the last few weeks of his Presidency.

The three of them sat over some coffee for several minutes making simple small talk. Then Janet excused herself and left Mark and Aaron alone.

"Aaron, first let me tell you how impressed I was with what you did in Texas. That took guts my friend – lots and lots of guts. But good for you! It was really the right thing to do. But what is happening now?"

"Well, sir, the President and his new Attorney General seem to be hell-bent on making life miserable for me, that's for sure. They are talking to the Grand Jury and apparently are trying to build a case that says I was the one who tried to get the votes fixed in Illinois strictly against the wishes of the President."

Mark interjected "Aaron, all I know is what I have seen on television and read in the papers, so I would like to hear it from you. Were you part of that business in Chicago?"

"No, sir, I had no part in that whole dirty business. When I heard what he had done I could not believe my ears. So, when he sent me down to San Antonio I decided I would just blow the whole thing up and reveal what had just happened not only in Texas but also in Chicago. And then I submitted my resignation. But, what I didn't expect was the retaliation against me. It's costing me a fortune to defend myself from what are absolutely totally false accusations. But I guess it just goes with the territory!"

"Aaron, that is exactly what my people told me to expect from you, and again, I congratulate you on having the guts to do what you did in Texas."

"Thank you very much. It means a lot to me to hear you say that."

"But, now for the real reason I asked you to come in today. We are beginning to shape our Administration, assuming of course that we are able to get over the electoral vote hurdle. I am very set on the idea that an Independence Party President should seek leadership from both of the existing political parties. Look, we have to get away from these fringe positions that seem to lock up the current parties. Obviously, I lot of voters out there seem to share a lot of the same values my team and I have.

"So, this is kind of a long winded way of asking you if you would be interested in becoming the Attorney General in my new Administration?"

There was a slight pause as Aaron looked directly at Mark Worthington, and then finally answered, "Sir, I would be deeply honored to join you and your team. I can hardly believe that this is happening, after what the President has been trying to do to me. I will tell you that my wife is going to be ecstatic about this – she thinks you are just about the best thing that has ever happened in American politics!"

"Well, I will certainly look forward to meeting her – hopefully very soon. And please tell her I'm very flattered to hear her opinion. But, also please tell her that I am absolutely delighted that her husband has decided to accept my invitation. I know that someone with the ability, the character and the backbone that you have demonstrated will be a very welcome addition to the Team Worthington."

With that said, Mark Worthington stood and took Aaron's hand in a firm handshake that sealed their understanding.

****

A couple of hours later Aaron Freedman pulled into his garage, and quickly moved into the house where his wife Pam was anxiously waiting for him. She had poured a glass of wine for both of them and sat at the counter in the kitchen. As the door from the garage opened she quickly rose and moved to greet him with a hug and kiss. He held on to her a bit longer than usual and she couldn't help but wonder if he had some bad news for her. She wasn't sure if she could handle much more bad news than they had been dealt over the last few weeks.

"Well, how did it go? Did you like him? What did he have to say about the President? Did you meet his wife? Did………"

"Hey, wait a minute!" as he raised his glass of wine and said "Cheers!"

She responded "Cheers" but now tell me all about it. Tell me, tell me! Damn, what are you waiting for?"

Laughing. Aaron said "I'm waiting for you to stop asking questions, if you really want to know. Yes, I did meet his wife and she is every bit as nice and gracious as she appeared during the campaign. And Mark Worthington is really something. He is as comfortable as sitting down with an old friend. He listens and smiles and asks good questions. He is just one helluva nice guy…..and"

"And? And what?"

"And he asked me to be the Attorney General in his new Administration!"

Pam's mouth dropped open and she just sat there looking at him for a full ten seconds when she got up and went over to him and put her arms around his neck and planted a real deep kiss on him. "Oh, Aaron, I am so happy for you! You so deserve this and to think it is offered even while the President is trying to screw you – wow! I am so proud of you!"

"Pam, the great thing is his dedication to building a team that crosses all kinds of lines. He really wants Independents. He wants people with character and people who are not tied to the old ways of thinking – the old ways of doing things. It is going to be a real treat being in on that. I really am beginning to think that this election is the closest thing to a democratically engineered revolution that we have ever seen. I am truly humbled to be asked to be a part of it."

Chapter 33

The executive committee of the Democratic National Committee was called to an emergency session by Chairman Wally Backstrom three days following the sudden resignation of Aaron Freedman as Attorney General of the United States. The meeting convened in the Headquarters located in the Watergate complex in Washington.

Wally opened the meeting by saying "The last few days have been breathtaking at best. None of us quite know what to make of the whole situation, but this I do know – the President no longer wants me to be in this position. That he made very clear at our last meeting at the White House. However, as little as he wants to do with me, I want less to do with him. We are all Democrats, at least we were up to the time of the election. We worked our asses off to get him re-elected, and we all failed to accomplish that. I'm still trying to figure out if the public rejected us because of our policies, because of the way we have been running the country the last few years, or because they have so little love for the President. Perhaps it is a combination of all three. A perfect storm if you will.

"However, it is certainly obvious that a great many of our office holders have abandoned us in favor of the Independence Party and Mark Worthington. Are they traitors? Perhaps. Are they realists? Perhaps, again. Will they return to us under new leadership and a new agenda? To me this is the real million dollar question. What is the future of this new Independence Party? Will it have any more staying power than say the 'Bull Moose Party' had. Or Ross Perot's party?

"Are we truly headed in the direction of an English Parliamentary system with at least three parties jockeying for control of the government?

"I wish I could stand here before you and tell you that I know the answers to all of these questions. But, I don't. Perhaps in time I will, but right now, I simply do not have any answers. So, I called you all here to announce my immediate resignation as Chairman of this great party I have belonged to all my life, and have worked so hard for all these years. We need new leadership and new ideas for the future. Otherwise, we will be the ones who go the way of the Whigs and the Bull Moose group.

"My final thoughts on all of this are these: we need to find someone who can think through all of these momentous changes and come up with a new and meaningful direction for this Party. We've got to put aside the tired old refrains of the New Deal, and the Fair Deal and all the Bad Deals that we have sworn allegiance to all these years. We have to start thinking about what the American people want and need and build our Party around that and not around a bunch of tired old clichés! With that I thank all of you for the wonderful years I have spent with you and I wish you all the very best as you move forward."

With that said, Wally Backstrom stepped down from the podium, gathered up his papers and left the meeting room. The very quiet Directors sat for a moment before the head of the South West Region stood and said, "I think we need to appoint a committee to begin a short search for a new Chairman."

The New York Chairman rose and said "I nominate that great American, Anthony Rosenthal, the President of the California Teacher's Union, to be our next Chairman."

With a quick second by the representative from the NAACP, a vote was taken. It was unanimous. And the Democrats marched on in lock step, as if nothing unusual had just happened outside the beltway.

Chapter 34

Bryce Randolph had just returned from his daily work out at the fitness center and as he entered the house from the garage, he was met by Jaclyn with a rather somber look on her face. "I'm just about ready to go to my painting class, but I think we need to have a little talk."

Bryce immediately began to rack his brain for what it was that he had forgotten to do with forgetting to call the landscaper or perhaps he had a thank you note to write. Whatever, the look on her face suggested that he was once again in some kind of trouble. He poured himself a fresh cup of coffee, and sat down at the breakfast bar. Okay, what did I do this time?"

"It's not what you did, it's what I'm afraid you might do in the future that has me worried."

Bryce thought to himself, "Ooo boy! Now I'm going to find myself in trouble for something I haven't even done yet?" So he smiled as casually as he could and said, "What am I about to do that I shouldn't do if I want to protect this 50 year old marriage that you and I have so carefully crafted?"

At that Jaclyn pushed a piece of paper across the counter – it was a phone number where he could reach Gordon Metcalfe, and a request that he call as soon as he got home. "Well honey, that doesn't look so threatening. Gordon is an old friend and probably wants to make sure that you and I are planning on attending the inauguration in January. Sounds like fun doesn't it?"

Jaclyn wasn't amused. "No, my silver-tongued friend, I don't think for a moment that that is why he called and left an urgent message for you to call. He wants something from you, and if you want my guess it will involve you getting on an airplane, once again, doing something for Mark or for the Independence Party. That's my guess, but I think you've done enough, maybe even too much, and I don't want to lose you for another six months on some 'urgently important matter'. I'm being a little selfish here, but I think I've given quite enough at the office, and I want my husband here with me and not off on some god-forsaken mission to anywhere in the United States. So, if I sound a bit peevish about this, well, I am peeved. So there I've said it!"

Bryce reached out as he had done hundreds of times in the past to take both her hands in his, but she shook him off, with a shrug that didn't need words to convey their meaning.

Jaclyn stood up and as she headed for the door, she looked back over her shoulder and said, "Do the right thing Bryce. Somehow or other I will accept it. But, just understand, I don't want to lose you again for months on end." She shut the door behind her with a bit more force than needed to affect a closure.

****

Bryce dialed the number on the message pad, and a couple of rings later, Gordon Metcalfe answered "Hello, Bryce, thanks for getting back to me so soon. It was good talking with Jaclyn a few minutes. Hope you two are enjoying your time together again."

"Well Gordon, it's funny you mentioned our time together, because I just got one of the worst tongue lashings of my married life from that beautiful lady about 5 minutes ago. And it concerned the message she had just handed me - the message to call you. She is not very interested, to say the least, in my taking on any more assignments that are going to take me away from here for very long. Now, please, old friend, just tell me that you were calling to offer me an opportunity to attend the inauguration or something really serious like that!"

Gordon laughed his good natured laugh, saying "Well, on the bright side, some letters are going to go out this afternoon to a very select group of people, including you and Jaclyn, from Mark. He absolutely wants to be sure that you will be coming to the inauguration, and all the parties surrounding that affair. By the way your invitation will include a very private dinner with just the members of the Inner Circle."

"Does that mean something has happened that we the unwashed don't know about?"

"No, no, no! But the uncertainty surrounding the final results is actually the reason I am calling you. We have done some extensive research over the last few days, concerning those folks known as Electors who will be casting their Electoral votes in a few days.

"Uh, oh, do I see some frequent flyer miles beginning to grow again for the Randolph family?"

"I guess you could look at it that way, but here's the thing. We have identified at least 15 Electors from a number of states ranging all the way from North Dakota to Texas that are clearly senior citizens, that is they are at least 65 years old. They are all party loyalists from way back, and that is how they were chosen to be Electors in the first place. But according to the statutes in their states, they are actually not totally bound to cast their ballot for the candidate who carried the state. Some of these folks are Democrats and some are Republicans."

"Gordon, you aren't going to ask me to do something illegal are you?"

"No Bryce, not illegal at all. As you may or may not have heard Mark has asked me to stay on and be his Chief of Staff, and I have agreed."

"Fantastic, Gordon! He could not have chosen a better person! Congratulations to you. But go on about these Electors?"

"Bryce, you did such a fantastic job in organizing seniors for us this summer, that Mark suggested we should call you and see if you would do this – I know – one more thing to help maybe get us over the top. We want you to meet with some of these people, and explain that they do not have a legal obligation to vote for either Bobby Houston, or for the President as the case may be. You have met Mark and know what a great person he is and you can convey that impression with a real honest conviction to these people.

"By contrast look at what their Parties are asking them to do. They are being asked to cast an all important Electoral vote for either Houston who is about to be indicted for alleged ballot tampering; or for the President who tried to buy people in Illinois to tamper with votes there. Now, isn't that a helluva choice for these poor obscure souls. Not one of them probably ever thought that this assignment was going to come down to making a monumental decision like this. But there it is!"

"Will you do that for us?"

"When is it – you know when do they deliver their ballots?"

"Their ballots have to be in by the middle of the first week of December. Then, they are opened in Congress the first week of January. So we have no time to lose – no time at all."

"This really was your idea wasn't it Gordon? Not Mark's."

"Bryce, I was not joking, nor being a total cynic, when I said that Mark suggested calling you. He really did. He is a real admirer of yours and feels confident that if anyone could convince a few of those Electors to change their votes, it would be you. Whaddya say, old friend?"

"Well, despite the fact that I know that I am going to catch holy hell in a couple of hours, of course I'll do it. And as you say the whole project will be over in a couple of weeks. So what's the next step?

"Meet me at the airport in Lincoln, Nebraska on Wednesday. We have booked a flight out of Sky harbor that should get you there about noon."

"Guess you were pretty sure I'd say yes, huh?"

"More than pretty sure Bryce. Damn sure!"

Chapter 35

Thanksgiving Week is always celebrated as a family holiday and it is no different for Congressmen and women. Most of the members of Congress have offices back in their home states but for a holiday like Thanksgiving they often choose to celebrate with close family members at their homes in the Washington suburbs. Actually this is one of the real problems with our representative system. So very many of our elected representatives have been in Washington so long they hardly think of themselves as being from Wyoming, or California or Ohio. No, they have lived in the rolling suburbs of Virginia so long they are far more comfortable there than back in the flat hills of Iowa.

But, this year was different. The Congress left, en masse, to get back to their 'homes' so that they could better judge what their constituents were thinking with all of this uncertainty surrounding the election of the President. They all had just won their respective elections but practically all 435 Representatives and 100 Senators seriously feared the fall out if they took a position in the turmoil which might be totally out of sync with what the people back home were thinking.

Molly Caldwell had just won her election race for only the 2nd time from her Dayton, Ohio District. She knew that being a Republican in this formerly Democratic district made her a real target in the eyes of her Republican supporters as well as her Democratic opponents; not to mention what the substantial number of independents in Ohio were thinking.

She spent Thanksgiving day at her parents home with the extended family including her husband's parents as well. The discussion at dinner was friendly, but intense, as she heard reports of how many people now wish they had voted for Mark Worthington instead of either Bobby Houston or the President. She had never warmed up to Houston very much, and she had a visceral dislike of the President which left her in a sort of 'no-man's land'. The newspapers in the state all the way from the Cleveland Plain Dealer to the Cincinnati Enquirer were loud and clear declaring "a plague on both their houses". They also were heaping praise on their own Ohio Senator Jeff Corcoran for having the intestinal fortitude to renounce his Republican Party affiliation and take up the Independence Party standard in support of Mark Worthington.

Molly had not gone as far as Jeff had but she came real close to following his lead. Her big decision now was whether she should elect to caucus with the Republicans or move over to the much smaller group of already declared (or even elected) Independence Party Representatives. At dinner as they all were settling back having coffee and some after dinner drinks she posed the question to the people she loved the most: her family. "Should I declare for the Republicans or should I go with Jeff and become a declared Independent?"

Everyone started to talk at once, but she put up her hands and starting to laugh, she said , "Whoa, slow down everyone. I'm not done telling you how I have thought this one out. If I leave the Republican Party, they will withdraw all support and will probably never welcome me back in case the Independence Party movement fizzles out.

"And that leads me to the next mine field. Can Mark and his small group of dedicated supporters in Congress - at least small for now – make this new Parliamentary form of government work. I know now that it wasn't always easy, but it seemed so easy with just the Republicans and the Democrats, and maybe an occasional maverick or two. But now with three! Is it possible that we can make this work without collapsing the entire system?"

At this point several people spoke up expressing their thoughts on the situation, including comments as to what they were hearing from their friends and neighbors and associates. There was no uniformity to the comments. Finally, the person she trusted the most and had always sought out when she had tough decisions to make, her Father, spoke up. "Honey, I think you did a good job of laying out the difficulties in making this decision, and you've heard all the comments from all of us here at the table. What I haven't heard is what you really think, deep down in your heart – and in your stomach. I have always admired and trusted your good judgment, and I would really like to hear what you think is your best choice!" As he finished speaking everyone around the large table nodded in agreement.

"What do I think? I think I got into politics in the first place because I thought I could help improve the climate in Washington, and I think, to some small degree, I have helped in that regard. I never saw myself as one of those birds that gets re-elected year after year after year, until they virtually forget where they are really from!

"So, I think, so what the hell am I worrying about what the Republican Party is thinking or what kind of punishment they may inflict on me. I think Mark Worthington is the best thing to happen to this country in a hundred years – so why not join him and his crusade to straighten out our country. Why not? What do I have to lose? If the movement fails and I get defeated – so what? I'll go back to my law practice and be happy ever after. If the movement succeeds and we can make this three party system work, then I am in on the ground floor and there is no way but up! That's what I think!"

Her Dad looked at her for quite a while and finally said, "That was what I wanted to hear you say, and I never doubted for a minute that you would figure it out just like that." With that he got up and moved around the table to her chair and gave her a big hug, and said "We are all so proud of you honey. I hope the American people find out soon what a real pro they have with you in Congress!"

Molly's husband, Randy, stood up beaming from ear to ear. Raising his wine glass he said "A toast to one of the finest Representatives in the country. My love : Molly!"

****

Meanwhile in states all around the country, similar scenes were being played out with other Congressional people soaking up some of the intense vibes that were pulsating through the country.

In Arizona, Hector Lopez was a newly elected Representative from one of the Phoenix Congressional districts, and he was getting an earful from a meeting with a group of his supporters.

"Hey, Hector, if the election goes to the House, who you gonna vote for?"

"Don't know yet!"

"Whaddya mean you don't know? You're a Democrat ain't cha?

"Yes, I am a Democrat but I am also a concerned citizen, and I do represent a lot of Republicans and Independents, even though they may not have voted for me."

"Whaddya know about Worthington? Worth-while or Worthless?"

"You know, I know about the same as all of you do. You watched the debates, and heard what he had to say about the major issues. And as far as playing on his name, my only comment to that is 'shame on you'! We don't need that kind of trash talk surrounding a Presidential candidate, especially one who very well may be our next President. So clean up your mouth, and be respectful of the office!"

****

Ronald Brown, a Congressman from a solidly Democratic district near San Diego had his staff arrange an impromptu (although scheduled well ahead) event in a public park near his California headquarters. After a crowd of several hundred had gathered Ron took the microphone and stepped off the makeshift stage and down into where the people were seated.

He began with "Y'all know that this is a pretty momentous time in our history. I recognize a few faces out there but there are a whole lot more that I don't know, so welcome to all of you. I would like to take a little informal and certainly not scientifically administered poll. How many of you think that as a long time loyal Democrat, I should support the President if the election actually does make it to the House of Representatives?"

He had them vote two more times: once for the Republican candidate and once for Mark Worthington.

"Well, it doesn't look like many Republicans showed up here today, but you certainly are telling me that between supporting the President and supporting one of the other two, most of you seem to think I should support Mark Worthington.

"I have to tell you folks, I have been in Congress for 20 years, and I don't believe I have ever been asked to make a more difficult decision. Do I support the President, the leader of my Party, the party that has supported and rewarded me for 20 years, now. Or, do I turn my back on the Party, and support one of the other candidates- I honestly have not decided yet, but I sure do appreciate your support and your comments."

"Would you have any trouble voting your conscience Ron? By the way what is your conscience on this one?"

The crowd laughed at that one, but Ron waited until they quieted down and he said "I'm not sure what my conscience is telling me on this business, but I will tell you I'm gonna be doin' a lot of thinkin' and pray-in' in the next few days. But hey, why don't we all go home and have some good old turkey? With that he turned and moved toward his car, as truly confused as ever by the many comments he had just heard.

****

Finally in Florida, under a beautiful late November sun, with the water of the Gulf of Mexico lapping quietly behind him, Representative Morris Mayweather III stood before a group of northwest Florida citizens who had come to hear some remarks from their newly elected Independent congressman.

"Mr. Mayweather, are you still happy that you switched parties to run as an Independence Party candidate, or do you sort of wish you had stuck with your old Republican party?"

"You know, that is probably the easiest question I'm going to be asked today" he answered with a big smile.

"Here I am, answering questions about where my loyalties will be in January if the Presidential vote goes into the House. I chose to run as an Independent and I support Mark Worthington and all he has stood for, 100%. I don't have to choose between voting for my standard bearer and someone who has just disgraced his party, as have both of the other candidates. That makes my decision easy. I will vote for and support Mark Worthington all the way, and be damn proud to do it."

Chapter 36

John Sylvester Marshall was not the kind of person who would wait around seeking a half dozen opinions before he did something that he sensed was the right move at the outset. He got on a plane and immediately headed to San Antonio where he summoned the Federal Attorney who was about to go to the Grand Jury with the indictment papers for Governor Houston. He also ordered the three mayors involved to come to the Federal offices to answer some questions.

Marshall addressed his first questions to Oscar Ramirez, the Federal Attorney from San Antonio. "Oscar, what made you want to call a Grand Jury and bring charges against Governor Houston?"

Ramirez was a bit taken back by the obvious implication of the question, but he quickly answered "The evidence was very clear, what with the tapes and all. The mayors all conveyed the same story to me, and your predecessor directed me to proceed. So I did."

Marshall then turned to Mayor Rodrique Costello, of El Paso and pointing his finger at the Mayor asked "Did you follow through on what the Governor is supposed to have asked? Did you in fact direct some activities to manipulate some number of ballots so that the Governor would be sure to gain enough votes to win the state?"

"No, I did not do any such thing."

"How can I be certain that you are telling the truth? That in fact perhaps you and these other two Mayors didn't actually mess with enough votes to compromise the outcome. After all the Governor did carry the state didn't he?"

They all nodded yes, that Houston had actually won in Texas but not by very many votes. The Mayor of Plano spoke up and said "I rather resent the tone of your questions, sir. We did nothing but report what the Governor tried to do to us, and we understand several others who have not surfaced as yet. We did nothing wrong and you are suggesting that we may have been a party to this damn thing. Frankly, that is an insult to me!"

Marshall continued, "Look sonny boy, you may flap your arms and sound all exercised about what I said, but I'm simply suggesting that maybe the Governor might have been joking about this whole thing, but that all three of you may have quietly fixed enough ballots that he ended up winning the state. In which case maybe I should direct Oscar here to also take *your* names to the Grand Jury as being willing participants in a plan that won the State of Texas for the Governor. How do you like that outcome?"

It was now Oscar Ramirez' turn to speak up, and he quickly jumped to the defense of the three Mayors. "I'm sorry to have to take issue with you on this, but these three guys did exactly what any law abiding person would hope and expect them to do. They refused to tamper with ballots or have anyone else tamper with them either. They reported it to me, and with the former AG's full approval I called for the Grand Jury to meet. Frankly I can't believe that this discussion is even taking place!"

"Well, it is taking place. And at the direction and approval of the President I am taking charge of this investigation and we are going to include these three miserable specimens in the charges that we will take to the Grand Jury. And you Mr. Ramirez have until 3pm this afternoon to clean out your office. I will send my FBI associate with you just to be sure that you don't try to steal anything pertinent to this case. If you wish you may submit a letter of resignation, but if I don't have that by 3 also, consider yourself fired!

"And as for you three, be prepared to appear before the Grand Jury in two days. But just get all of your miserable selves out of my sight right now!"

****

Oscar Ramirez quickly left for his office, and the three mayors were right behind him. But unfortunately the FBI agent who had accompanied the Attorney General was also right there as well. As he began gathering up his personal belongings he saw his Administrative Assistant in the door, and he said, "Sorry about this quick exit, but I have been directed to leave my office by three. I'm not sure who is going to replace me, but for now the Attorney General of the United States seems to have taken charge of the San Antonio office. Please let every one know that I have not and will not resign, but have been summarily fired by the Attorney General, supposedly at the direction of the President of the United States. Please let as many people as you can know what I said."

He then turned to the three mayors and said, "I will see you in the lobby – hopefully around 3:30. Hope you all can make it!"

Chapter 37

There is nothing more certain than the fact that politics are rarely played according to any rules associated with gentlemen. What is particularly peculiar, one might say an oxymoron, is that so many politicians play golf – the ultimate in a gentleman's game. But, then, perhaps they cheat on the golf course as well!

So, what the political stew in Texas on this day included is a President who is half crazed because of his most recent political failures; an over the top attorney general who is an interim appointment and subject to virtually no oversight; and a Texas Governor who went completely off the deep end when he lost his bid for the Presidency. This all adds up to a 'political feast' for even the modestly interested followers of politics.

Governor Bobby Drew Houston arrived back in his office in Austin quite late in the evening, although he had notified his secretary and a handful of his closest staff to be in the building when he arrived. Because it was late on a Saturday night it did not appear that there were any people from either the Press or the Media hanging around, so he was able to sneak in unnoticed.

Once in his office he had his secretary call the others in for a quick update. "Okay, where are we folks? I've been away a few days, and haven't heard too much of what is going on. But, I understand that an indictment against me has been handed down to the Federal Grand Jury. Is that correct?"

Scott Witherspoon his young Chief of Staff spoke up first. "To begin with all hell is breaking loose down here. I guess you know that you will be served papers tomorrow that were ordered by the new Attorney General John Sylvester Marshall."

"Whatever happened to the other guy – what was his name – Freeman or something?"

"Aaron Freedman resigned right before he would have been fired by the President when he said he was going to bring the President before the Grand Jury in Washington for the crimes he ordered the people in Chicago to commit."

"Okay, okay, so what about me?"

"As I was saying, the new guy is bringing you up before the Grand Jury down here because of what you tried to get the various Mayors to do.

"But in addition to that he is also going to ask the Grand Jury to bring charges against the Mayors of El Paso, San Antonio and Plano, on the grounds that they may have conspired to tamper with ballots even without your involvement. He's going after all of you!"

"Holy shit! You gotta be kidding me. What's this all about? What in the hell is going on?"

"Well the best we can figure out, the President has ordered the new AG to stop the business with the Grand Jury in Washington concerning the President. It now appears that just as a few Congressmen seem to be gearing up to start impeachment proceedings against the President, he has decided to take the offensive and cause as much trouble for us as he can. By doing this he is also causing trouble for the Republican Party as well. It is sort of one of these, 'if you are going to try and destroy me,

I will destroy you at the same time. It's Armageddon, but with one survivor, Mark Worthington!"

"Well, isn't that just dandy. So, what does it look like for me around the state?"

Everyone got very quiet, until Scott answered, "As sorry as I am to report this, it looks like you are pretty well ruined. The polls all show your popularity at about 8%, and most of the major political players around the State have given statements distancing themselves as far as they can get from you. Really sorry to have to tell you that.

"One piece of gossip that you probably missed while you were away is that Jimmy Foxworthy's wife has sued him for divorce, and even his bimbo girlfriend now says that she doesn't want anything to do with him either."

"He is one useless piece of crap. I probably would have won if I had picked anybody other than him. So do you have any more good news you want to lay on me?"

Scott stood up and said, "No, but before I leave here tonight I would like to make one suggestion?"

"And what might that be?"

"I think you should seriously consider resigning, preferably tomorrow before any indictments are handed down. It could take the sting right out of the grand jury deliberations, and might lead them to say 'so what' and let's get on with the running of our state under the new Governor.

"Actually, I think the reason Marshall is taking the mayors to the Grand Jury is to use them against you. So, no matter what you might testify to, he'll have all three or even four mayors telling essentially the same story which severely implicates you. So all the more reason to bail now and take the gun out of his hand!"

"In other words drink the hemlock and move on! I'll think about it. But while I have you all here I do want to thank all of you for sticking by me and the office while I was away. I also want to apologize to all of you for what I did – it looks like I really screwed up and I'm really sorry for that. But I do appreciate all that you did for me and my family, and I'll let you know what I'll do tomorrow morning."

Chapter 38

If you had told Steve Marsh a couple of years ago that he would be getting ready to meet with several other young Representatives to consider bringing impeachment proceedings against the sitting President of the United States, he would have laughed long and hard. But here he was about to drive to the House office of his friend Mitchell Briggs to do just that.

Steve turned to his wife and said, "You know what honey? There are times when I think about how uncomplicated being President of the Holland school board was. That seems like a hundred years ago and now look at us. Are you enjoying this trip? Am I enjoying this trip?"

Marcie moved around the kitchen bar and put her arms around Steve's neck and drawing him very close she gave him one long and loving kiss. "Now, does that tell you whether I am enjoying this trip or not? How can I even begin to tell you how it feels watching you develop into the person you've become over the years. Our boys and I are so proud of you, we are just bursting! Of course we are enjoying the trip, but I do have to ask you about this impeachment thing. Do you really want to do this?"

Steve gently released her grip and led her to one of the four bar stools and he then sat down facing her. "I have some mixed emotions about this whole thing. I think the President was dead wrong in what he did, and I think he really did commit a crime which should be punishable by impeachment and probably losing his office. But then again it is going to be such a distraction for all of us, including the President and his people. He lost the election badly, he has now pretty well disgraced himself, and now we're going to force him to face impeachment charges? I want him to be impeached but I just can't help thinking that maybe with just a few weeks left, maybe it just isn't worth it!"

****

Mitchell Briggs was almost completely recovered from the wounds he had suffered at the hands of a would-be assassin a few months before, and now he sat having coffee with his wife.

"I'm real nervous about this whole thing Corrinne. There is so much maneuvering going on in Congress right now that I can't decide if this is the right thing to do now or not. We really don't know how we are going to organize a Congress with *three* major parties – even how to seat them becomes a problem. But how do committee heads get picked? Do we have to align with one of the other parties to create a majority which none of us will have at the outset.

"Then there is the heartburn about how everyone will vote if no one gets the number of electoral votes needed to be President. Now we are going to throw in an impeachment on top of all that! God, how much can we be expected to deal with in just a few weeks?"

"Honey, I hear all that and I know it's heavy for you and all the rest of the people, but that isn't what is worrying me the most – not by a long shot."

"Really! What is it?"

"Some crack pot took a shot at you back in California and I'm scared to death that someone is just lurking out there ready to try again. You were lucky the first time, but will you be that lucky again?"

190

As Corrinne began to tear up, Mitchell got up and put his arms around her and said, "Nothing is going to happen to me sweetheart. That really was a crack pot that took a shot at me. No one here even knows who I am, much less wants to take a shot at me. Please don't get upset. I really need you right now! I really wish I was just a little stronger because I am really feeling the pressure. What I will tell you is I'll be damn glad when the next few weeks are history, and hopefully Mark is the new President and we can all get back to something like normal. Although, now as I say that, it really sounds almost like a joke. I'm not sure we will see 'normal' again for a long time – if ever!"

Mitchell continued holding Corrinne in his arms, and finally gave her a long, gentle kiss. He then picked up his ever-present brief case and left through the kitchen door to the garage on his way to the Capitol.

Chapter 39

At the very same time that Mitchell Briggs and Steve Marsh were saying good bye to their wives, Mark Worthington, Gordon Metcalfe and Jamie Gonzalez were meeting for breakfast in a conference room at the Willard. After they were served three very different breakfasts, Mark said, "I want to note that this will be the first of what I hope will be a great many breakfasts and meetings between the three of us. As I have told you both separately I want this to be an 'Office of the President' if you will. Of course the ultimate decision on every issue will always be with me, as it should be. But I want totally open and frank discussions between the three of us. If you disagree with me, or with each other, then I want you to speak up and tell me what is bothering you. I don't expect that we will always reach a consensus among us, but whatever decision we do make will leave this room as though we all have agreed. Are we all good with that?"

Gordon spoke up first. "I am simply overwhelmed that you are willing to open up to us and let us give you our opinion on issues, and I can assure you that once the decision is made, it will be *our* decision!"

Jamie then added, "You know a lot of people warned me to avoid the Vice President's job, saying it held the curse of being buried alive in Washington D.C.! But, what you are proposing we set up here is so far removed from that I can hardly believe my ears. And of course I will pledge that once we come to agreement I will treat that decision as if it were my very own."

Mark Worthington then continued, "Great, I think we are all starting on the same page, and that really sounds good to me.

Now, for the first thing I have on my mind is how do we deal with this movement on the Hill to launch impeachment proceedings against the President? Gordon?"

Gordon thought for a moment and said, "Honestly, gosh, I guess that everything I say in these meetings better be honest, so I'll rephrase my comments" with which Mark and Jamie actually laughed out loud.

Gordon continued, "I think we and the members that we have 'some' control over, that is the people elected as members of the Independence Party, have far better things to do over the next few weeks than mucking around with Impeachment proceedings. The President has had anything but a distinguished Presidency these past few months, and now he has committed what is no doubt an impeachable offense. But his Presidency, his reputation, his place in history - they've already been sealed. Why bother wasting the time of the Congress and the money of the American taxpayers to simply put another exclamation point behind an already badly stained and failed Presidency. I say let it be, and let's move on to other much more important things."

Gordon turned to Jamie who said, "As much as I would like to apply the final 'coup de grace' to that miserable son of a bitch across the street, I totally agree with Gordon. He is done, ruined, disgraced, so let's let him sit there for a few more weeks and then slither out the door taking his pension and Presidential staff with him. No one will listen to him in the future and it will be like he was never in the oval office. Good bye, and don't let the door hit you on the ass on the way out!"

Mark chuckled to himself as he summed up the discussion. "I agree with both of you. No matter what we may think of him personally, he is still the President of the United States, and despite the stupid thing he did a few days ago, let's continue to have our side stand on the side of human decency, and just leave him alone. He is all alone in that office right now, with just about no one supporting him in any way. The American people showed their lack of respect and concern for him in the way they voted, so why do we need to kick him now.

"Gordon, I would like you to call those fellas that are gearing up impeachment papers and respectfully ask them to back off starting any kind of action like that. I fully expect that at least one Congressional committee, probably in both Houses, will open an investigation into his actions, so let's just leave it at that. Will you take care of that for me Gordon?"

Gordon's final comments were "Actually, if we advise all of the people who are officially *and* unofficially with us on the Hill we probably already have enough votes that the impeachment process would be doomed to fail, so why bother with it. That may be the very first real effect of having an Independence Party!"

****

Gordon Metcalfe left the meeting and called Mitchell Briggs, Steve Marsh and some eight or nine other Congressmen and women and relayed Mark's wishes. All but two of them were frankly relieved to get such a message, and readily agreed to back down from such precipitous action.

Mitchell Briggs summed it all up when he observed, "You know what Gordon? I'm honestly relieved to get this kind of direction from the top because frankly I don't think the Congress should be wasting its time trying to impeach this guy. All that would do is make him think that he is still really important, and he really isn't important any more. He is a poor excuse as a person, and an even worse excuse for a President of the United States. Let's not spend the next two months putting his face on the front page of the news. I'll work on putting a lid on this whole thing."

Chapter 40

Although the political parties in the United States have grown progressively more partisan and further apart on issues over the last 50 years, there still remains the urge to compromise on the part of many legislators. Senator Ellen Livingston was one of those centrist minded people. As a matter of fact she felt so strongly along those lines that she became the only female to mount a credible Presidential primary campaign earlier in the year. Unfortunately for her all of the rest of the wanna-bes, with the exception of Mark Worthington, ganged up on her. They wanted no part of her moderation.

When Ellen finally realized that she had a like minded soul mate in Mark Worthington she was no longer reluctant to drop from the Presidential primary race and strongly recommended that all of her fervent followers take their primary votes and get behind the General with the same passion they had supported her. This was nearly enough to swing the nomination to Mark at the Republican convention. But when Bobby Drew Houston made some kind of deal with Jimmy Foxworthy which finally carried the day with the delegates, she was one of the first legislators to heartily endorse Mark Worthington for President on the Independence Party ticket.

Ellen felt so strongly about her beliefs that she too renounced the GOP and registered as a member of the Independence Party, on whose platform she ran for re-election. Now she was meeting for the first time since the Monday morning press conference in Texas with Bob Madison and nine of the ten Senators who made up their bipartisan group fondly known as the Mavericks. They had been evenly divided between 6

Democrats and 6 Republicans in the last Congressional session. But now they found themselves to be 4 Democrats, 4 Independents and 4 Republicans.

They were in Ellen's office this time, as per their long established custom, the host was entitled to set the agenda and act as the moderator.

"Well guys, here we are. Since you all are here I *think* I can assume that we still qualify as *mavericks* – am I right?"

There were several chuckles and many smiles as they all acknowledged that they still considered themselves to be moderates, and not extremists within their respective parties.

The Senator from Wyoming spoke first. "Ellen I see the only item on the agenda today has to do with how the Senate is to be organized. Even though we are still the very same people today that we were six –eight – twelve months ago, things are really quite different today. We are no longer meeting on what I considered neutral ground – the middle – somewhere between the loonies in my party and the crazies in the other folks camp!"

This observation got a full throated laugh from everyone. But, he continued, "this really means we aren't on neutral ground anymore, because, for one thing, here we are meeting in the good offices of the Senior Senator from New Jersey, member of the newly minted Independence Party. So what are we supposed to do now?"

Bob Madison took up the challenge. "I would say that all of us who haven't already declared for the Independence Party should make that decision now, and elect to vote with the I Party in organizing the Senate, but even more to the point I think we should all choose to sit with the rest of the I Senators, demanding that we be seated in the middle of the floor between the other two Parties. That is what I think you and I and all of the rest of us here should do!"

Another spoke up saying "Aside from those of us in this room, how many Independence Senators are committed today?"

Ellen responded, "Aside from those in this room, there are six Senators who either ran for election on the I ticket or have switched their Party registration to the Independence Party. I might add that there appears to be between 65 and 70 Representatives in the House who will also be demanding to be seated as Independents, as well."

There was an audible sigh and silence that enveloped the room with that assessment. These twelve men and women knew the high stakes game that they were playing. To leave their respective parties in favor of Mark's team could mean one of two extremes. They were either going to join the wave of the future, under a bright, charismatic leader, or they were committing political suicide for their future fortunes. Obviously the respective parties they had operated with through all these years were not going to take too kindly to them hoisting a new flag. It was a big, a very big bet, in a deadly serious political poker game. What to do?

Two of the members of this moderate group that had been meeting now for some 10 years pushed their chairs back and rose as if to leave.

"As much as I respect all of you, and what you have stood for all these years, I am simply too old to abandon the Republican Party at this juncture. I have two years left and I just can't make this move this late in my life. But I will promise you that I will vote to seat you all as a separate group. I think you also know me well enough by now that I will continue my moderate approach to our country's problems. I wish you all well, and I guess I'll see you in January when we open the Electoral ballots." With that the oldest member of the mavericks, both in age and in time with the group, quietly left the room.

That left one more Senator standing. "I'm 65 years old and have been a Democrat all my life. My Daddy was a Democrat and state Senator back home, and my son is a Democrat and in the House back home. I might be wrong, but I fear that the backlash by the party should I decide to defect might well wash right over my whole family – and I just can't let that happen. My gut is telling me to join up with you Ellen, and the rest of you fellas, and maybe after a few months or a year from now, I'll decide, what the hell, let's do it! But right now, I just can't take the chance. I too will support how we seat you all and you know that I am honestly a moderate at heart, and always will be. So, maybe for now I can do more for the cause of moderation if I just continue working within the Democratic Party than if I abandon them. I think I just have to take that chance.

"But just because we now have an Independence Party doesn't mean that we have to quit meeting with each other, does it? We still have so many of the same goals for the most part, I say let's keep getting together occasionally as we try to impose some sanity to some of these crazy political issues. But with that I too will have to say goodbye." With that said, he moved around the table and embraced Ellen fondly, and shook hands with Bob Madison; then left the room.

With 10 members of the Mavericks left around the table, Ellen said, "I certainly agree that we don't have to quit meeting just because we have a new party – how about the rest of you?"

As Ellen suspected there was no disagreement about their continuing to meet. But, what was perhaps the biggest surprise of the day was when the remaining 6 Senators, one by one, rose to declare that they were resigning from their respective political parties and were casting their lot with the Independence Party.

Ellen thanked all of them for their support and the courage that it took to make this change. "We are all jumping into some really murky water right now, but somehow or other I think we are really making the right decision. I think when the history of this period is written it may well be said of us 'brave souls' who chose to risk everything for the sake of their principles. What greater legacy can a person leave?"

They all raised their glasses in salute to this challenge.

Chapter 41

For all the hoopla associated with Presidential elections in this country, or for that matter in any real democracy, they are really just a means to an end. The voters decide to vote for one candidate or another based on a lot of fairly innocuous criteria. Do I think he is good looking enough to be President? Do I like the way he talks – does he reassure me, or does he challenge me, or does he simply put me off? Do I really believe all the negative campaign ads I heard or saw? And finally some voters vote because they are white and their man is white; or they are black and their man is black; or they are a woman and their candidate is a woman. These are really important issues to a lot of people – perhaps far too many people!

Then there are those who actually listen to what the candidates said they are for: silly little issues like do they want to raise or lower taxes. Or do they seriously want to create jobs, or do they just want the economy to continue drifting. Or do they believe in a woman's right to choose, or do they believe women have no right to choose what they do with their body. Then there are those who seriously want to get people off welfare and into jobs, while there are others who simply want to keep funneling money to the people who can't or won't go to work.

The number of issues seems to be endless and there always seems to be two sides to every single issue. When there were only two major parties in the United States people were forced to side with one or the other, even though their particular political party may have taken a position one didn't agree with.

So this election season upset the usual balance where you either ended up on the Left or on the Right. Suddenly there was a middle – some people who positioned themselves *between* the two extremes, and *their* man won the most popular votes and the most electoral votes and is likely to end up in the Oval Office.

Mark Worthington was the man in the middle. He had grown tired of deadlock in the government caused by the two extreme parties, the Liberal Left and the Conservative Right and all the baggage that both sides were forced to carry. During the campaign he had discussed a wide range of important issues during the Presidential Primary campaign, and then again as he ran as a true Independent for the Presidency. He won almost enough electoral votes to be elected outright, and he had far and away the most popular votes among the three candidates.

So, now Mark was gathering with his innermost circle of advisors, including his newly appointed Chief of Staff and his running mate to discuss just what issues they were going to vigorously pursue at the beginning of their administration (of course assuming that they were going to come out the winners in the very up in the air electoral process.

"Without seeming to be too overly proud, it seems to me that the voters of this country have certainly looked with a great deal of approval at a lot of the things we talked about during the election. Do you all agree on that premise?"

Jamie spoke up first. "I think that we can assume only one thing for sure, and that is that the American voters liked you a helluva lot better than those other two – even before the others revealed their true colors. And I would suggest that their 'colors' as such are probably black and white stripes, if you get what I mean."

Jeff then added "Actually, I agree with Jamie. But being the most popular candidate doesn't necessarily mean that you have a mandate to carry out every one of the ideas you talked about in the campaign."

Gordon then followed up "That is fundamentally true. Even among all these independents who saw fit to vote for the Independence Party candidate, there are large numbers who lean heavily to the left, and probably an equal number who lean heavily to the right and then somewhere near 50% who agree with all of your talking points right down the middle."

"So then what does that lead us to?"

Mitchell Briggs suggested, "I think that it should lead us to pore over all these issues real hard, and come up with maybe four at the most that we can really sink our teeth into – and start lining up support in Congress and in the media for these ideas. I look back on some of the great Presidents in the past, who told the public 'these are the four things we are going to concentrate our effort on right now, and we are going to bust our asses to get good solid legislation together and get it passed!'"

Gordon then warmed up to the subject by saying "I would also like to suggest that our administration should break with the hoary old tradition that we have to present these bills to Congress immediately and demand action in the first 100 days. For God's sake there is nothing sacrosanct about the first 100 days, and as a matter of fact a lot of bad legislation has been passed because of this hurry up and act atmosphere – no matter how badly done it is or even how unconstitutional it may be. Look at old FDR and all the crap he got passed in exactly 100 days, and then had to stand by and watch as the Supreme Court took it apart, piece by piece. I'd say, let's tell the American public that we are going to seek meaningful legislation on four specific areas and we are going to allow ourselves and our partners on the Hill six months to get the work done right! What do you all think about that?"

Mark had been listening attentively to this exchange and when there was finally a pause he said "I like that a lot – I think that will show that we are serious about these things and that we are going to be deliberate in our crafting of these bills and we will expect the Congress to be equally deliberate in their consideration of the bills. Yes, I really do like that approach!"

Jeff Corcoran joined in with "Fantastic, Gordon- a new out of the box, independent candidate wins the election and immediately breaks with tradition and sets a steady deliberate course of action – allowing six months to get it done right."

****

The five men continued to talk through lunch and into the early evening when Mark suggested they adjourn and meet again in the morning. He summarized their work so far: "It looks like we have some degree of consensus on the issues that we should consider and from which we can select 'the big four' for our six month push. I see:

1. Immigration reform

2. How to repair all entitlement programs including Health Care and Social Security

3. The Economy and creating jobs

4. How to deal with the increasing burden of the national debt

5. Improving Education, public, and private

6. How to upgrade our deteriorating infrastructure

7. Our role in the world including how strong our military should be

8. How to deal with the issue of terrorism, both Domestic and International

Mark looked around at everyone and then directed his next question at Senator Jeff Corcoran:

"Jeff will you and Mitchell gather up 6 or 8 of the most thoughtful Congressmen – and women you know – maybe some of that Maverick group I've heard so much about - and ask them and their staffs to work on a position paper or two related to possible legislation regarding these six issues, and hopefully sometime in the next 3 or 4 weeks we can call them all together and see what they managed to come up with. God knows we are going to need their help once we start proposing legislation, so let's have them take a crack at some of these right now. It will sure help us to reach our goal of 4 carefully crafted, meaningful pieces of legislation in our first 6 months!"

"Do we want folks from our Party only working on this?"

"Oh, no, not at all! Let's try something really innovative here and see if we can get some input from all sides and work from there. Unless I'm missing something from the election results I think that is really what the people out there want us to do."

Mitchell Briggs then added "I think you've got a great thought Mark, but I'll tell you where the real problem is, and it is buried in every one of those items."

The room got very quiet and they all looked at Mitch waiting to hear what he had to say.

"Folks, each one of these areas of concern cost a lot of money, and just like with our own personal household budgets, I'd really like to take on all of these and 4 or 5 more. What do we propose doing about improving the lot of all our minorties, what to do about finding cures for cancer and Alzheimer's disease, what about our rapidly aging population? You know these are big, serious issues, but I'm certain we just can't go after all of these things right now. But I think we should begin researching the next 8 or 10 major issues and at least let people know that we are not impervious to them, but that from a financial *and* time standpoint we just can't do everything at once. But we will get to them as soon as we can."

Mark summed it all up "Mitchell, that was said like a true statesman, and of course you are right. So perhaps our first priority will be to prioritize our long list of objectives and try to figure out what absolutely has to be done first from a need standpoint and from a financial doability standpoint. These need to be addressed and done in the next six months! The rest will just have to wait until later!"

Chapter 42

As the door to his office swung open, the Mayor of Chicago rose from behind his enormous desk to greet Jeremiah Brady. "Jerry, it's really great to see your ugly face. I hear you had a bit of a tough go of it in the White House?"

"A bit of gallows humor", Jerry thought as he reached for the Mayor's outstretched hand. "Well, if you consider your ass chewed out by the President and then getting fired, I guess that was a bit 'of a tough go."

"Jerry, I'm supposed to hear today what the President and his new Lord-high Executioner has in mind about the little scandal we almost had here a couple of weeks ago. And frankly, I have not a clue in hell what to expect from the visit. In any event, I packed a toothbrush and a change of shorts in case they handcuff me and carry me out in my chair…"

Jerry had to laugh at that image. "I dare say that won't happen."

"Oh, I don't know. It seems to me that the Prez has sort of come unglued over the past few days. I'm not sure what anyone can expect from him these days."

"Well, I'd be hard pressed to argue with you on that but do you think he will actually go after you considering what really happened and what we *all* know he did?"

"My gut feel is he'll back off on taking me to a Grand Jury, because he is afraid of what will come out – who knows I might even produce a tape that could be very, very damaging to our little man in the White House!"

"Yea, I think you are probably right. I suspect he wants to divert as much attention away from himself as he possibly can and just hope that he can survive until January 20th. The last thing he wants is an impeachment to deal with."

The Mayor peaked his fingers and looked rather wistfully out the window on his great city, and said, "You have a point there. His ego is under severe duress, shall we say? He hates the idea that he is an 'accidental President' but he sure as hell doesn't want to compound that with having to defend himself in an impeachment hearing. Well, enough about his majesty. Let's talk about Jeremiah Brady. Have you thought about what you are going to do next?"

"Well, yes and no. I know for absolutely, positively certain I will never work in the White House again – I don't give a crap who is President or what party he belongs to!"

The Mayor started to laugh saying "Hey pal, I know just how you feel. I've suffered through my share of Ovalitis and I just want to settle in right here for the next few years. No Governor, no Senator, no Cabinet position – just leave me alone right here in this great town!"

Looking around the room, Brady observed "It looks to me like you might just have the best job in politics, maybe even the best job anywhere."

"Yea, I really think so, too. But anyhow, Jerry how would you like to work for me? No goddamn neighborhood organizer or whatever they call that useless job. I'd like you to be one of my special assistants, doing a lot of ground work around town and being my in house polling expert. I always need to know how I am doing – you know there are always elections to be won. But beyond that what are people saying about me and about the town. What is it they really want? What is it they really like? What is it they don't like either a lot or a little? I can get out and talk to people anytime I want, but I've been around long enough to know that most of the time people will tell me what they think I want to hear! That's all well and good, and it serves to feed my ego just fine. But, look Jerry, I need someone to get under all that bull shit and lay it out for me the way it *really* is. And that is where I see you. You have the polling experience; you work well with the ordinary folks and I *know* you aren't afraid to pull on the King's goatee. And that my friend is what I want from you. Are you game?"

Jeremiah Brady thought about this offer for about 15 seconds and then he accepted "Long live the Prince! Long live the great city of Chicago!"

****

At promptly 1100 the interim Attorney General of the United States, the Honorable John Sylvester Marshall was led into the offices of the mayor of Chicago. He strode rapidly across the office and greeted the Mayor with a firm handshake. With a bit too much bravado Marshall said "It's a pleasure to meet you sir. As much time as I spent in Washington over the last 20 years I don't know how I managed to miss you especially in and around the White House. But better late than never!"

The Mayor smiled a typical politician's smile – one that said I don't have a clue who you are, and I really don't like you very much – all at the same time. But he was also thinking, "I know I met you about four years ago, but then I was a mere bit player

209

in the greater Oval Office scene, and you wouldn't have paid even a little bit of attention to me from your 'exalted' position as a member of the steering committee of the Democratic National Committee." He also thought, "I didn't like you the first time I met you and I like you even less today."

"So, I'm sure you are anxious to know what message I am bringing from the Justice Department."

"Indeed I am quite interested in that message."

"Well, to begin with, the White house staff has been working the phones really hard the last few days, and I want you to clearly understand that we think we can win this election in the House. Even though Our Man somehow didn't get as many votes as the other two, we think we can carry 26 states in the House and actually create a bit of a miracle for the president."

The Mayor interrupted "You've got to be kidding – you aren't serious, are you?"

Marshall's face got very red, very suddenly. Veins popped out on his forehead and in his neck as he responded "Look my little prick, I'm not in the habit of small town politicians like you telling me that I don't know what I'm talking about! So you better sit up in that oversized chair of yours and listen up! We think we are going to win this thing, and we want as few distractions out there as possible. And frankly, you are a distraction – a miserable, minor one to be sure, but a distraction none the less.

"So we've decided to drop any charges against you and against Aaron Freedman as well. Talk about your minor league players, he had no more business being Attorney General than you would have being a four star general!"

The Mayor took advantage of Marshall taking a breath and said "Well, that is all very gracious of you. Has anyone told you recently that you are imminently qualified for the 'son of a bitch of the year award'?

Marshall smiled with close to the most malevolent smile that the Mayor had ever seen. This led to Marshall responding "I don't really give a good god-damn what you – or anyone else – think of me. My total allegiance is to the President and, by the way, the Democratic Party. For the next few weeks we're playing hardball, for all the marbles if you will. And we can't be bothered by small time chump change like you and Freedman.

"But, if you have any brains at all in that melon head of yours then you better be sympathetic to the President and work your ass off over these next few weeks to be sure that the President gets the support he needs to win in the House. Getting a majority vote from the Illinois delegation would be a good place to start. If you opt out of supporting the Man, or worse yet, get negative about him or try to influence legislators against him, we'll know about it. And when we win this election, you'll be hard pressed to get coffee money from the Federal government – understand me?"

The Mayor stood up and took a short step toward Marshall and even though he had to tilt his head back to look up at him, in a very firm voice said "I understand you perfectly well, and I would like you to take a message back to our exalted President – the accidental President I might add. And the message is this: "Go straight to hell! I can't imagine, in my wildest dreams, that I would lend my support to him and the miserable human beings he has chosen to represent him. Now, please get the hell out of my office and don't let the door hit you in the ass on the way out."

Chapter 43

Bryce Randolph arrived in Sioux Falls, South Dakota around 3 in the afternoon, and was met at the airport by Jack Whitney who had been Mark Worthington's chief proponent during the months leading up to the election. Unfortunately, the President carried the state by less than 450 votes. The state is small with only 3 electoral votes, but with Mark Worthington needing only 8 electoral votes then these 3 votes could be huge.

Whitney brought Bryce up to date quickly. "I contacted all three of our Electors and there is good news and bad news. The guy from Rapid City let me know in no uncertain terms that he is a Democrat, and has been a Democrat all his life, and there is no way in hell that he is breaking with the party now, or ever. I think that was pretty close to an actual quote. When I asked him if he was proud of 'his Man's behavior' since the election he said something like "what behavior?" and then he hung up on me."

Bryce laughed at the description of the conversation and said "So is that all the bad news or is there more?"

"No, there is actually some good news. The other two will be here tomorrow morning – one at 8 and the other at 10. They were definitely surprised to hear from me, but they were really quite interested to hear what you have to say tomorrow. I hope it isn't a waste of time for you to puddle jump in here just to see these two folks."

"No, no, no! We're down to looking for 9 more electors to come over to our side. With the 262 we already have that is all we need to avoid all this messy business in the House. So, 1 or

2 from here and one or two from a couple of other states and we can make this thing work for us. So, no, it is not a waste of time. I am just grateful to you Jack for being able to get these two birds in here so quickly.”

✳✳✳✳✳✳✳✳✳✳✳✳✳✳✳✳✳✳✳✳✳

Alec Brown arrived well before the appointed 8am time, and when he saw Jack Whitney he stood and moved quickly to greet him. He had known Jack for a great many years and had the utmost respect for Jack Whitney’s political integrity, and even though they had been in opposite political camps recently they had an obvious warm feeling for each other.

“Hi, Jack! It’s really good to see you. So who is this guy that is going to put the strong arm on me this morning?”

Jack laughed and said, “Well, his name is Bryce Randolph and he is about as far removed from being a strong-armed bully as you can get in politics! He was the guy you may remember was rounding up votes for the Republicans by organizing Seniors all over the country.”

“Oh, yeah, now that you tell me that I do remember him. He did a helluva job getting senior support for the Republicans. But didn’t he quit and go over to Mark Worthington after the Convention? Just like you, I might add!”

“You got it. And, he was pretty damn successful in getting a lot of those folks to line up behind Mark, too – unfortunately not quite enough in South Dakota as it turns out. But here he comes now and since he's popping for breakfast I'll let him take it from here."

Bryce also greeted Alec warmly and the three of them sat down for a bite to eat. Bryce began by saying "Alec, I really appreciate you taking the time and making the effort to meet with me this morning. I don't know how much Jack has told you about my mission – so to speak – but it is really quite straight forward.

"Mark is 8 electoral votes short of winning the election outright, and I'm doing some quick leg work in the central part of the country to see if there are some Electors who might be uneasy about who they are nominally committed to vote for."

Alec put his fork down, and carefully wiping some toast off his mouth he responded, "I know that I am not 'legally' bound to cast my vote for the President but it is my understanding that there have been damn few Electors who ever – and I mean ever - switched their vote to another candidate."

"You are absolutely right on that one. There have been very few incidents of this happening, but it has happened. But, here is what we are asking you to think about. Mark Worthington won the popular vote by a very large margin, but because of the quirk in our Election System, he is 8 Electoral votes short of being the President-elect right now.

"But even more important than that fact, is what has happened *since* election day. You're a Democrat and the President is a Democrat, and I dare say you are a long time Democrat of some substantial standing, or you never would have been designated an Elector."

With a vigorous nod Alec showed Bryce that indeed he was quite correct in that assessment. But then Alec surprised Bryce with his next comment. "But what you don't need to remind me of is what the President tried to do with the Illinois votes. Talk about disappointing! I never really liked him very much but I figured what harm can the little prick do as Vice President. But, then comes one heart attack, and he's now the Man! Unbelievable! But then to try and get the Mayor of Chicago to rig the votes so that he could carry Illinois? Am I in some kind of dream, and will it all go away when I wake up?"

Bryce spoke in a very quiet voice "It is pretty unreal, but you are not dreaming. His own Attorney General was going to bring him up before a Grand Jury, but I understand that he fired that guy and got his new guy to stop that action. What can I say?"

"There are only three of us here in South Dakota, and I have no idea what the other two will decide to do, but I am thinking real seriously of voting for Mark Worthington. I'll tell you that right now. But I do have to look at some practical things as well. If I do that, my goose is cooked as a Democrat. And that rotten bastard down in Texas would keep me from ever going over to the dark side, so if I have any political life left at all, it would have to be as an Independent. Tell me, are you offering me something to do this?"

Bryce looked him straight in the eye and said, "I am not offering you anything but a chance to help do the right thing and put the right man in the White House, the man who far and away got the most votes. If you decide to join the Independence Party Mark and the others will welcome you with open arms. But other than offering you an opportunity to do the right thing for the American people, that's all there is on the table."

"Alec stood and offered his hand to Bryce saying "That is a very fair and honest offer. I guess I kind of expected that response from Mark Worthington. I won't commit to anything today, but I will promise you that I will give it a lot of serious thought – a lot of serious thought."

****

Bryce Randolph and Jack Whitney had a somewhat similar meeting later that morning with the third and last Elector from South Dakota who expressed similar negative thoughts toward the President, but who was far more concerned about his political job, and the effect on his long term employment should he abandon the President right now. He would not go as far as Alec had gone in committing to serious thought about switching, but he did say that he would weigh the possibility along with all the other things that he had to consider.

On the way to the airport, Jack asked "Where you headed Bryce?"

"I'm off to Illinois. They have a lot of electoral votes, and they are all committed to the President right now. My man Reggie Tate is going to meet me and as of late last night I think I will be able to talk to at least four of the electors tomorrow. So we will see what we will see. How did you think these two sessions went this morning?"

Jack responded "I thought you did a masterful job, of making it a conscience thing, rather than a political decision. How in good conscience could you vote for that bastard – and no, we are not in an Electoral Vote buying mood. Do what's right for the country, and if you want to come over to our side, hey, we'll be happy to welcome you. Period. Over and Out"

Chapter 44

Puddle jumping through the Midwest at any time of the year is no one's idea of a fun experience. The aircraft rarely get to an elevation even as high as 10,000 feet and often are as low as 4,000 feet. The aircraft are small, often less than 50 passenger turbo jets, and the ride is bumpy and choppy at best. But Bryce Randolph was used to it, and he was smart enough to know that he had to carefully watch what and how much he ate before boarding one of these wonderful flying machines. A quick lunch of a large bratwurst dog with a bag of chips was simply out of the question. And as much as he hated a steady diet of leafy greens with a little tofu thrown in, he found himself eating more like a rabbit during these short hops.

In Illinois the Worthington front man was able to set up appointments with six of the twenty-one Electors. Four others had flatly refused to even consider meeting with a representative from the Worthington camp.

Reggie Tate had been a long time moderate Democrat from down state Illinois but he was one of the first from that party to defect and get on the Mark Worthington band-wagon. After the appropriate greetings Reggie opened with "Bryce, it's good to see you again, and I hope you have some success with these old boys. Actually old boys and old girls as it turns out since two of the Electors do happen to be women.

"Almost without exception these folks hold some position in state or local government. Some were elected and many were appointed. They were picked as Electors because of their presumed loyalty to the ticket and to the party. And four of the people I contacted reacted pretty strongly – almost outraged if you will – that we might ask them to listen to an 'enemy' representative."

Bryce's immediate response was "Well, there is no harm in asking them to listen to what we have to say. Did any of them give a reason why they wouldn't at least talk to us?"

""Oh, yeah! They all said something like 'You know what would happen to our jobs if we talked to another party about our vote? The reaction would be quick and certain. We would either be fired or rejected by the Party at the next election. And they all said that they just couldn't afford to risk losing their jobs."

Bryce responded "I sympathize with them – believe me I do. And what is even more difficult is that I am not talking to them about any quid pro quo. I'm just suggesting that they may want to consider the merits of the three men they *could* vote for and make a courageous decision to buck their party for the possible good of the country. No promises, no jobs, no payoffs – just vote your conscience.

"It's interesting Reg, I've sold a lot of things in my life, and this is at one time the easiest thing I've ever had to pitch and also the hardest. These are hard core members of their political party who owe everything to that party, including their livelihood. But here I am challenging them to consider voting against the man who is the head of their party at this point in time. And I am basing that on the behavior of the man over the past few days. I can tell you for sure that I would have a hard time myself coming to grips with a decision like that!"

****

The third person that Reggie Tate introduced to Bryce Randolph was Erma Lindholm, a 60-something widow who served in the appointed position of County Clerk in her downstate county. She was an extremely energetic and well groomed lady who obviously had fought her share of political wars and managed to win more than her share.

"So, Mr. Randolph, I understand that you want to talk to me about how I'm going to handle my vote for President. I must say that I've been an Elector a few times in the past, and never had the experience of someone actually coming and talking to me about how I was going to vote."

"Please, call me Bryce. I would much rather that than Mr. Randolph. Would that be okay?"

"Sure, Bryce. I would like that – and I am Erma. Now tell me what your offer is."

Bryce laughed and said "Erma, I don't have an offer, and as strange as that may sound, I am only here to appeal to you to consider how you vote in light of what is happening right now. The fact of the matter is our candidate, Mark Worthington, is short about 8 electoral votes of being the next President. In fact if Mark had carried Illinois he would be he President-elect right now, and I would not have had the opportunity to sit and chat with you today. But he fell short by a few hundred votes in your fair state."

"Guess that means we did a pretty good job of getting out the votes for our man, doesn't it?"

"Yes, indeed it does. But, we want you to consider the fact that the President only got a little over 30 electoral votes, which was a pretty strong repudiation of the man. But then the things that happened right after the election with his very own Attorney General trying to get him before a grand jury concerning his trying to strong arm the Mayor of Chicago. Well, Erma, it just isn't a pretty picture. So, we are simply saying if only 8 Electors like yourself would have the courage to buck the Party apparatus, and vote for the man that obviously won the most popular votes, then the country can avoid all the drama and the angst of the election going into the House. Would you consider doing that?"

"Mr. Randolph – I'm sorry, Bryce – I will admit to you that I never thought I would ever consider such a proposal as you just made. But, the fact that you are not trying to bribe me or threaten me in any way really gets to me. You want me to put my conscience before my party affiliation. What an interesting political concept that is!"

"That is it exactly Erma!"

"Well, Bryce, again as I say, I will consider it. But you must know that there is a lot more goes into a decision like this than just a little bit of conscience salve, and I have to weigh those considerations as well. But, I promise you that I will give your idea a whole lot of serious thought.

"By the way you know that nothing has been proved as yet about what the President has been accused of doing?"

"For sure I know that. But it may be months before that works itself out in the courts. And right now, we don't have months. We have a few days before those Electoral votes have to be turned in. And that short time frame is exactly what we are up against."

Erma stood up, and she moved right in front of Bryce and shook his hand vigorously. "Thank you Bryce. I really appreciate your visit, and you make a very persuasive point, and as I said, I will give this a lot of serious, and prayerful, attention."

****

After Erma left the room Reggie Tate brought in five more Electors who had agreed to meet with Bryce. The results of these discussions ranged all the way from a "Hell, no, I won't consider doing that!" to a couple of strong emotional responses suggesting that the respective Electors were having a very bad time in anticipation of having to cast their vote for a man they thought might be on the verge of being impeached. No promises, no pledges, but just a lot of serious interest with a commitment to 'think about it'.

"Well, Bryce, where you going now? Cook County or where?"

"Reg, I'm catching a flight to Dallas from here. Texas has a whole bunch of electoral votes, and we feel that surely there must be a couple or more who are fed up with the Governor and his vote-grabbing behavior. So, I'm headed to Big D to see what kind of interest I can drum up for Mark Worthington.

"But, thank you Reggie for all your help. I think we may have uncovered a couple of diamond nuggets today. But, we'll just have to wait and see."

Chapter 45

A great majority of citizens across the landscape of America probably think that their Representatives and Senators are far off in Washington working from sunup to sundown on the affairs of state. And most of these august centurions that they have sent forth to do battle with the great issues of the day do spend a good bit of time with their nose to the legislative grindstone.

But they also spend huge amounts of time meeting and greeting constituents from back home in Flagstaff, Arizona or other similar far-off points in their home states. Then there are the lobbyists to be seen and listened to, and the damnable committee meetings that must be attended. Occasionally, and only occasionally there will be a floor call and they might have to show up at their desks in their respective chambers.

So, how much time is left. Well, there is quite a good bit of time left for such pleasures as eating: lunch and dinner are favorite times of the day for these folks because they can get by cheaply in their respective cafeterias for lunch, and all too often they are entertained at dinner. There is the occasional golf match at any number of prestigious clubs around the greater Washington area, and plenty of tennis and handball for the more athletic members.

But what of their families? Do they ever see their families or are their many 'duties' so demanding that their wives, for example, might have had a more satisfying social life had they stayed in Boise? Well, it turns out that they do have a social life and a rather full one at that. Not only are the couples wined and dined frequently by the well heeled in Washington, but they also manage to carry on the more subdued socializing associated with get-togethers with good friends, both in and out of government.

Jamie and Cissy Rodriguez had gotten to know Jeff and Nancy Corcoran during the Presidential campaign just past, and an immediate bonding took place. They managed to see each other as couples about every two weeks, and the women saw each other even more frequently. Jeff was a veteran Senator by now, and Jamie had been Mark Worthington's vice-presidential running mate. Jamie had a lot to learn about the Senate and Jeff was a most willing and able mentor to him.

Before inviting John and Pam Black to join them for dinner at their suite in the Willard Hotel, Cissy made sure that the Corcorans understood that John was a journalist, and that he was writing a book about this Presidential election. Linda relayed a positive thumbs up to Cissy and the plans were made for a wonderful catered meal by the world-class chef in the Hotel.

They all enjoyed a Cosmo before dinner and one would have thought they were all long lost friends. John was particularly relieved since the highest ranking officials he had interviewed previously were a few Representatives from his home state. Jamie and Jeff were intrigued by the idea of a book based on the meteoric rise of Mark Worthington and the Independence Party in national politics and were most definitely excited to help John with background material on what got Mark to the White House or at least almost to the White House.

Jeff stressed the fact that Mark Worthington was not just a flash in the pan who came out of nowhere to be chosen the country's leader. "Mark had an extraordinary academic background culminating with the earning of a Ph.D. Then his military portfolio was almost the perfect story - first in his class at the Point followed by one outstanding assignment after another until he got to the top. No, this was no fluke. He had all the credentials a voter could ask for!"

Jamie then added "Not to mention he is an extraordinarily likeable person who simply lights up a room the minute he enters it."

Jeff continued "Jamie, that is absolutely right on. I think the American people are going to be in for a wonderful learning experience once he takes office – and I am totally convinced that he *is* going to win this thing one way or another."

Nancy added "And John, I hope that you get to meet his wife someday. She is the perfect complement to Mark – just a wonderful lady. She has no political aspirations of her own but simply wants to support him in whatever he wants to do. She has raised some great children and I'm sure she'll make a great spokesperson for some wonderful program or other. Maybe more than one!"

John then followed with "Well, who do we owe for bringing him out of seclusion and getting him into the national spotlight? I understand he was happily parked in Champaign as a guest lecturer at U of I – that is a pretty big jump!"

Jeff took that one. "Gordon Metcalfe is the man who convinced him he had to take on one more tour of duty."

"A king-maker in the great tradition of Mark Hanna and right out of Ohio, too!"

"Good for you John, I see that you know your American political history. Since I have the distinction of being from the great state of Ohio, I can truly appreciate the likes of Mark Hanna. But Gordon Metcalfe is really a cut above Hanna I believe. Do you know his background?"

"Well, I know he was the Chairman of the Republican Party for awhile, although I think he was replaced during the primaries wasn't he?"

"Yes, because he was trying to bring some sense to the party. He couldn't stand the choice between Houston and Foxworthy. He really liked Ellen Livingston but the party was not about to turn to a woman when they had such great good-old-boys to choose from. Gordon is a moderate, and he wanted someone with moderate credentials to lead the party. And they chose to execute the messenger instead!"

"Jamie, how did you get in the picture?"

"I too am a moderate. From an important state – Florida. And I have a Hispanic last name. Lucky, I guess!"

"And he just happens to be damn good looking, and smart as well!" was Cissy's contribution.

They all got a good laugh after that. The dinner was served and afterward Jeff advised John "Get in touch with Jimmy Foxworthy if you can, and see what he can tell you about the primaries, and what happened to him. Also call on Ellen Livingston, a great lady in her own right, and see what she has to say about the way she was treated by the various contenders. And if you will put together a list of questions I'll see what I can do to get Mark to answer them for you. I can't promise to get you in to see him, but I'll do the best I can. I really wish you the best of luck in getting this all together.

In all seriousness, this election looks like a watershed in American politics. If you can capture that theme you'll have a sure-fire best seller on your hands and quite possibly a Pulitzer prize to go with it."

John then asked Jeff, "Is there a big money man hidden in here somewhere?"

"Great question! and you really need to highlight this area. Our politics have been so dominated in the last few years with the Koch's and George Soros' of the world that the voters have become really turned off - but Mark's money came in small bills from 1,000's of donors - sort of a moderate Bernie Sanders - a really genuine grass roots support!"

Chapter 46

Bryce Randolph always enjoyed flying into Dallas going all the way back to 1979 when the Airport was brand spanking new and it was possible to park your car right outside most of the terminals. How things had changed over the intervening years as the Airport developed and grew into the mammoth operation it was today.

But this time he would not have to find a parking place because the Worthington advance man, Charlie Carson, would be picking him up at the gate. Charlie was a long time friend from business dealings many years before, and ended up being easily recruited to help run Mark Worthington's late developing campaign in the great state of Texas.

Charlie embraced Bryce with a big bear hug and a "Welcome to Texas Bryce! I hope we can make some big things happen while you are here."

As they left the gate area Bryce confided to Charlie that he had some hope of success in both South Dakota and Illinois, and that maybe it wouldn't take too many converts in Texas to get them over the top.

****

The first person that Charlie introduced to Bryce was from El Paso, and just like the Mayor of El Paso he was a 5th or 6th generation Mexican American whose family lived in the Texas territory long before the Mexican American war. Sam Alito spoke first. "Mr. Randolph, I understand that you are here to find out if I still intend casting my vote for Bobby Houston. I'll tell you what. On the day after the election I had no doubt in my mind that I would traveling to Austin in December where I would proudly cast my vote for the honorable Governor of the State of Texas!

"But then look what happened in just a few days of the election. The Governor proved without a doubt that he really isn't *honorable* – but rather he is a despicable bigot, and what is worse he was willing to commit a crime to secure a few votes! Can you believe that he would stoop that low?

"I will tell you something right now. There are 4 other Electors who are long time descendants from pre-American control of this state. We are proud Americans! Yes, we are also proud Texans despite the fact that some of our ancestors may not have wanted to be Texans at all!"

With that Sam gave a small laugh and a shrug of his shoulders.

"Well, then Sam, I guess Charlie and I are wondering what your plans are?"

"Well, as I said, I've been in touch with the other four and we discussed what to do. We thought about just not voting – as a sort of passive vote of protest. But then we figured that really wouldn't do anybody any good. All that would happen then would be Bobby would get 5 fewer Electoral votes, no one would win the election and then it would go to the House of Representatives and that son of a bitch might actually end up getting elected President. How about that for one rotten turn of events?

"Then to tell you the truth the next thing that happened was Charlie called and said he wanted to set up a meeting with you to talk about our votes. Are the other guys here too?"

Charlie nodded affirmatively and said "They are all down the hall waiting to talk to Bryce."

Sam replied "I rather thought they would be here. Why don't we save you and Charlie a lot of time and just have them all come in here where we can all hear the same story. I think they would all like that."

Bryce stood and said to Charlie, "Why don't you go get them – I really like this idea."

****

Besides the four close partners to Sam Alito, there were two other Electors who also came in to meet Bryce. One of these was from Plano and the other from San Antonio.

There were a lot of handshakes and greetings all around before they all sat down and turned to Bryce.

"Well, you all know why I am here and what I want to talk to you about. But before you even ask, here is the deal - *there is no deal!* I am not here to offer you anything in return for your consideration of switching your vote to Mark Worthington.

"Mark says that this administration is not going to stoop to the level of both Bobby and the President to get a few votes. All we have to offer is this: a chance to vote your conscience; to vote for the one man who has emerged from all this as a clean honest candidate who just by the way got far and away the most popular votes and almost enough electoral votes to win the whole thing outright.

"As hokey as this might sound that is the kind of opportunity that not many people will ever get in a lifetime of political service. Additionally, we will welcome you with open arms should you decide to go all the way and join up with us in the Independence Party. No jobs, no money, no guarantees – just the chance to do the right thing for our country."

With that Bryce took a drink from his coffee and waited for the response. The first to speak up was the Elector from San Antonio who said "I know where some of these other folks are coming from and I want you all to know that I truly appreciate the 'non-offer' you bring. The Mayor of San Antonio did the right thing in resigning and turning in the Governor, and I certainly don't want to see my vote wasted and allow even the possibility of the President sneaking back into office through a vote in the House of Representatives."

Then the Elector who lived in Plano repeated practically the same speech, and looked expectantly toward the other 4 who were listening intently to what was going on. One by one they repeated how disappointed, even disgusted they were with the way the Governor had treated the Mayors, but in particular Mayor Rod Castillo. But they went one step further and pointed out that the new Attorney General was now going to bring these four Mayors before the Federal Grand Jury as possible participants in this massive vote fraud that the Governor had instigated.

As one of them said, "What a crock of shit that is! That's our crooked President lashing out at these Mayors who should be treated like heroes, not taken before a grand jury!"

Charlie then looked around and said "Does that mean that some or all of you intend to cast your votes for Mark Worthington?"

One by one they all 7 confirmed that was exactly what they intended to do. Bryce stood and shook hands with all of these Electors and thanked them from the bottom of his heart for their courageous decision, and once again thanked them on behalf of all the American voters for what they intended to do with their votes.

****

As soon as the meeting broke up and Charlie and Bryce were left alone, Bryce picked up the phone and dialed a number in Washington. Gordon Metcalfe answered "Bryce, I'm really glad to hear from you. How have your meetings gone?"

Bryce was almost a bit giddy as he replied, "Gordon, they could not have gone better. We have seven Electors in Texas who have committed to Mark, one in South Dakota who is leaning hard toward that decision and 2 in Illinois that I think will come over to our side. That is 10 in all, and I think that will be enough to tip the election to Mark. Isn't that right?"

Gordon said, "Hold on just a second Bryce, I want to give the phone to someone who will be really happy to hear your report." With that Gordon gave the phone to Mark Worthington who listened with obvious keen interest as Bryce reported his results.

"Bryce, we can't thank you enough for what you've been able to do. It's a real tribute to your persuasiveness!"

"Well, Mr. President, and I use the title advisedly, I would beg to differ with you a bit. I didn't have to be persuasive – I appealed to the conscience of these good people and merely

pointed out what a great person they would now be voting for!
And that was really easy."

Chapter 47

Just a little over a year before Chad Henson had been the very successful Chief of Staff of Senator Jeff Corcoran. Unfortunately when Jeff began a preliminary look at the possibilities of mounting a campaign for the Presidential nomination, he found out that Chad had some very serious policy issue differences. When faced with these differences Chad was implacable and forced to resign.

But nonetheless Chad remained on a friendly basis with the Corcoran family and when he was married Jeff and his wife were pleased to accept an invitation to the wedding and reception. In the meantime Chad had taken an important position with the campaign team of Texas Governor Bobby Houston. Chad was a Washington insider and Houston learned a great deal in the short time he employed Chad.

Unfortunately for Chad shortly after Jimmy Foxworthy announced that he was giving up his long campaign for the Presidency directing all of his delegates to support Bobby Houston Chad had a major falling out with the Governor who rather summarily dismissed him.

Now with all the uncertainty surrounding the results of the election and what was going to happen to all three of the candidates, Chad called Jeff Corcoran and asked if he could see him right away. Jeff recognized the urgency in Chad's voice and agreed to a meeting later that evening.

****

Jeff was sincerely interested in what Chad was doing now that the election was over. "You left Bobby Houston's team even before the convention didn't you?"

"Yeah, I did. I just couldn't stand it one minute longer. You know, you and I had some fundamental differences of opinion way back when we first started talking Presidential talk, and later when Bryce Randolph sent that manifesto to you."

"That's right Chad, and believe me I hated it when it came down to you having to leave us here. You were one great Chief of Staff and that was one of the hardest things I ever had to do. Believe me!"

"Well, I only mention it because as difficult as it was for both of us, it was really the right thing, for both of us. You are as honest as they come and I think of myself as being a decent person. But let me tell you, Bobby Drew Houston is not an honest person. He has virtually no scruples at all, and it just got worse the closer he got to the nomination."

"I sort of gathered that all along Chad, and I wondered how you were going to get along in that kind of cesspool. I really did think of you several times and I just shook my head. Honestly, I was damn glad to hear that you had left him."

"What I really wanted to tell you was what happened to Jimmy Foxworthy. I'm not at all sure that anybody outside the very inner, inner circles of those two guys really ever knew why he dropped out so unexpectedly – and so quickly at that!"

"Well, I do know that Mark and I, and Gordon Metcalfe, speculated quite a bit, because of course that practically guaranteed the nomination for Houston. And I might add, it was what led Mark and Gordon to decide to form the Independence

Party and go it alone. And you know what? That hasn't worked out too badly so far!" They both smiled and laughed quietly as they recognized the obvious understatement from Jeff.

"So, why did Jimmy bow out, besides the fact that he was running way behind in raising campaign money. Did he go broke, or God-forbid, did Bobby see to it that he was paid off?"

"Well, he was running low on funds, no doubt about that, but he wasn't broke and as far as I know he didn't get any money from Houston. But as I understand the circumstances, it was pretty well known that he was sleeping with that big blonde that led all the singing at his meetings – did you ever see her?"

"Oh, yes, I did run into her a couple of times. She sure could make heads turn but she was hardly my type. I couldn't help but wonder why she always seemed to be with Jimmy, but his wife hardly ever made an appearance."

"To show you what kind of slime bag Bobby was he managed to get cameras into Jimmy's bedroom at the Convention Hotel and he got some really graphic pictures of Jimmy jumping his sweetheart. So he called Jimmy in and told him he had two choices: drop out and pledge his delegates to Bobby, or face complete humiliation and be forced to drop out – a totally disgraced human being. What choice did he have? He caved and the rest is history. Bobby got the nomination, and Jimmy went off and campaigned in the back woods never to be heard from again."

"How many people know about this Chad?"

"Not too many – a couple people very close to Bobby's campaign."

"Does Jimmy's wife know?"

"She does now. And that is why she sued him for divorce. She literally kicked the ass-hole out of the house. I happen to know Jay McCauliffe really well, and when he finally got the whole story he was as angry as I've ever known him to get. He knew that Jimmy was banging that broad, but he didn't find out the rest of the story until after the convention. He wasn't sure what to do considering he would be in line for a big job, working for the Vice President, if Bobby managed to somehow win the election. But he quit a few days ago, and he says he doesn't want any part of politics anymore – no way, no how!"

Jeff just shook his head saying, "Can't say that I can blame him for that kind of decision. But, tell me, why are you telling me all this right now?"

"Well, Jeff, I thought somebody in Mark's corner needs to know about this – how do I describe it – this sordid mess. Because, what if, in some bizarre way Bobby should end up winning the election – you know, if it goes to the House and he gets enough states to back him. It's bad enough what he tried to do with the ballot fiasco, but can you imagine having a President who got nominated by illegally videotaping another candidate making out with a campaign worker - who it just so happens was not his wife – and then blackmailing him to drop out? It's enough to make you want to throw up!"

"I think someone may have to have a long heart to heart talk, sort of down and dirty with Mr. Houston very soon. The American people should not have to face the possibility of either one of these trash bags having a shot at the Presidency. The country deserves a whole lot better than that!"

Chapter 48

There is an old saying in the Advertising business that bad publicity is better than no publicity at all, and Governor Bobby Houston was a firm believer in that adage. He called his campaign staff together just a day or so after he admitted his errors in the ballot tampering affair, and he announced a change of heart.

"We haven't lost this race yet, and we still have a chance in the House. No one in their right mind is going to vote for the President after the $10,000,000 suitcase incident. By the way where is that money now? Did he get it back or what?"

"No one seems to know what happened to the money, Bobby. He probably got it back and shoved it back in the oval office closet. Hope he did a back ground check on his cleaning staff."

At that all of his advisors got a good laugh. Then Bobby continued "I want you to get our best phone people busy right now calling every damn one of those Representative who are going to vote in their state delegations. Tell them if they will vote for me their vote will not be forgotten. If they waffle a little, then tell them I will call them right away and repeat my pledge to be loyal to those who are loyal to me. Isn't that the political way of life in America? Now isn't it?"

It took several hours to get everything set up, but by dinner time the most seasoned telephone reps were reaching Representatives all across America with the same message: Bobby Houston wants and needs your vote in the House of Representatives, and he wants to know what he can do for you to make that happen?

✳✳✳✳✳✳✳✳✳✳✳✳✳✳✳✳✳✳✳✳

In the meantime Jeff Corcoran had taken a walk away from his office in the House Office Building, and as he often did when he was struggling with an issue he found the fresh air to be therapeutic in getting his thoughts straight.

"We just can't let these two scoundrels be in a position to become the President so what is the best thing to do now?"

He soon had his answer and it all began with a call to Gordon Metcalfe. "Gordon, how soon can you get Mark and Jamie together? I have some information they need to hear and I have a plan that may just resolve this dilemma and possibly win this election for us. Call me back on my cell."

✳✳✳✳✳✳✳✳✳✳✳✳✳✳✳✳✳✳✳✳

Gordon was able to arrange a meeting for 5pm in their temporary conference room at the Willard, and he reached Jeff on his cell phone to relay the arrangements.

Mark was particularly fond of Jeff Corcoran not only for the effective work he had accomplished in the Senate, but because he had been so supportive and worked so hard campaigning for Mark in the election. The fact that Jeff was an all-around nice guy just added to his positive assessment.

"So, Jeff, you called this meeting - what have you got for us?"

Jeff wasted no time in reviewing what he had just found out about Bobby Houston and the Jimmy Foxworthy affair. He made it clear that he thought that Houston had probably done something illegal, especially regarding the tape and the blackmail, but that he had some concerns about just how to proceed at this point. But he knew that Mark would want some options so he laid it out like this: "We could go to the new Attorney General John Marshall and dump it in his hands. He has already gone to the Grand Jury in Texas with the ballot tampering scheme but he seems hell-bent on not only destroying Bobby but also trying to destroy the Republican Party in Texas – by going after the mayors as well.

"Or perhaps a couple of us should make a quick call on Governor Houston, and point out what we know about his campaign and what he did to sew up the nomination. Then we could give him a couple of choices – none of which he'll like very much."

"Like what choices?" Mark asked.

"Resign the Governorship immediately. And by direct communication, release all the Electors who were supposed to cast votes for him, urging them to do the respectable thing and cast their votes for Mark Worthington.

"If he doesn't like that option, then consider the fact that we will go public on all the national networks, plus CNN telling what we know of his actions, and suggesting that additional charges (no doubt criminal charges) should be brought against him for illegal videotaping and for blackmail.

"Additionally, I wouldn't be surprised that we might even get Jimmy Foxworthy to come forward and tell the whole ugly story of what Houston did to him and to his campaign. So not only would he be ruined politically for the rest of his life, but his personal life would no doubt end up right where Foxworthy's did – in a divorce court."

Jamie Gonzalez let out a low, extended whistle as he summed up his feelings "Those are two pretty tough options, Jeff. Do you want to shoot yourself with the pistol we are offering you, or do you want to jump out of the window we just opened for you. What a stupid ass!"

Gordon commented "I don't know, but I think I would be running as fast as I could down the hall toward that window before you decide to close it on me."

Mark had been deep in thought up to now, and he offered, "This is all well and good Jeff, but really should we offer him this easy way out? Doesn't hiding what he did then make us a party to the whole sordid mess? Won't this come back and bite us in the butt six months from now – right when we are about to finish our first round of legislative fights. Someone will find out about this – Bob Woodward, or someone like him, or maybe someone on Foxworthy's team, or maybe the bimbo, or maybe one of their wives will testify in divorce court about what happened. Then everyone will all look at us and say, if you knew, are you any better than they are? You've just been covering up the illegal activities of a political scum-bag. Do we want to be put in that position?"

"Mark, I'm honestly embarrassed right now. You have pointed us in exactly the right direction. It's the politically astute direction, but it is also the moral and honorable way for us to handle this. Our country needs more honest and straight talking leadership and what you just laid out is exactly that. Maybe with you leading the way our new Third Party Movement can take the high road and begin to force – or shame – the other two parties to shape up and be honest with the public for a change. Talk about a breath of fresh air blowing across Washington – this could force a whole new type of behavior on a town whose institutions are crusted over with lies and deceitful activities. "I'm sorry, but this just takes my breath away!"

Mark continued, "Thank you Jeff. I didn't think of it being quite as profound as you have suggested, but maybe you are right. Perhaps we can start out right now making sure that we always take the honorable course in everything we do. We don't want to be known as the folks who always take the politically expedient step, but that we are the people who take the right step for the entire country. Not everyone will agree with us, but by God, they will know that we are acting in good faith on their behalf!"

****

After the rest of the team left the room Gordon and Mark sat down to do some serious planning about this latest revelation. Gordon began "Mark I think we need to contact Houston and see if we can set up a face to face meeting as soon as possible."

With that said Gordon proceeded to lay out a plan to deal with the Bobby Houston situation and hopefully with the Electoral ballot shortfall. Mark listened attentively and after a few questions and some useful suggestions Gordon was sent out to start the ball rolling on a new approach to wrapping up this whole mess.

Chapter 49

The White House staffers could hardly believe how totally the new Attorney General, John Sylvester Marshall, had taken charge of all activities surrounding the Oval Office. There was no Vice President and all of the other Cabinet members had shrunk down to the size they were before they took their exalted offices – a roomful of academic nerds and political hacks that owed their entire existence to this one man. Marshall couldn't wait until the President's reelection was finally confirmed and they could fire the whole damn lot of them.

The President now found himself totally under the Attorney General's sway: the AG spoke and the President listened. The President might just as well have been disabled by a stroke because he could find no words to question this strong man. If this had happened in one of the Middle Eastern or African countries, the AG would probably have sent the President into exile and declared himself the temporary President. But this *was* still the United States of American and there were laws about such things.

Marshall spoke first "Here is where we are right now. First of all you won so few electoral votes we don't have any chance in hell to get enough of those votes to win. What we have to do is guarantee that none of the Electors defects – becomes a 'faithless voter' as the saying goes. We know that Worthington has people contacting a lot of Electors and planting that seed in their head. We are also contacting our few Electors reminding them that they run a very great risk if they should decide to bolt the Party. Frankly at this point I don't think it's the Democrat's Electors that we have to worry about.

"It's the Republican Electors that are in play so to speak and Worthington may just be able to swing enough of them to get the eight more votes he needs. But we just have to hope that he isn't successful. The first thing we have to do is leak the idea to the Press, in particular the bloggers who generally favor us, that Worthington's people are offering huge incentives if the "unfaithful" switch their votes. Doesn't make any difference if it is true or not, just plant the seed of doubt, and then lie through your teeth as you deny any culpability. That folks is the way modern day politics work - and we are desperate! Everyone understand?

Our biggest worry right now is if and when the Election gets into the House. How can we manage to carry 26 of the 50 delegations. There are some solid, long time Democrats in practically every state delegation, so we need them to stand fast and support you right down the line. Our folks have contacted every one of them and without boring you too much we have promised a lot of goodies to keep them in line which again we will deny swearing on our grandfather's Bible.

"But here is the really tricky part: the House vote will be done by the newly seated Representatives and with all those Independents the split in a lot of states gets us a lot closer to carrying a bunch of states. So we are staying clear of the new Independence Party gang and concentrating on the Republicans in the new House. We are offering them a lot of incentives – too many to mention – to vote for the sitting President, and not some smart ass General with a Ph.D. who rode in here on a great white stallion. We think we have reached and turned at least a few of them. So, to sum it up, we're working on the new Congress and hope that nothing happens in the Electoral vote."

"When will we know about the Electoral vote?"

"The Electors get together in their state capitols on December 17th. Electors in a little over half of the states are pretty much bound to vote for the candidate who carried the popular vote in the state. But there are something like 24 states where they aren't bound to do that and that's where it gets sticky. But, anyway on the 17th they meet and they declare what their vote is. So if there is going to be any defection that word will leak out really fast. And of all the damn bad luck both Illinois and Texas allow defections."

"So what do you think it really looks like John?"

"I think that historical precedent says no one is going to get the needed 270 and the election is going to the House – that is what I think."

"Good, good, good. Good work John. Keep working on those Representatives – and don't forget I know where there is a lot of money "laying around" so to speak, just in case you need it!"

"Mr. President, I would suggest you forget about that stuff and don't EVER bring it up again. Someone is already holding a big bag full of cash that you came up with and that little caper could come back and bite you in the ass big time. I am still trying to find out who has that suitcase, because I'm pretty sure that Aaron Freedman passed it on to someone, probably in the AG's office, but no one seems to know anything. But if I find out who did it……" and with that he took his right hand and quickly drew it across his throat."

"Okay, okay! I don't have any cash and have no idea where money might come from. Good enough?"

"Good enough – I think!"

Chapter 50

The following day after Bobby Houston had tried to energize his staff into sticking with him, he announced that he and his wife were going to fly over to Naples, Florida and spend a few days at the home of some old friends who had a substantial water front estate and who offered it to Bobby anytime he wanted to 'just get away'. There was a full time staff at the place and large walls surrounding the nearly three acres of waterfront property.

What Bobby didn't tell the staff was Mark Worthington and a couple of his staff were also going to fly into the Naples airport and would be meeting with him at 8pm the next day. Since the law called for the Secret Service to cover all three candidates, these plans had to be made very quietly. Fortunately the secret service is part of the Homeland Security Office, and at the moment there was no one sitting in that particular Secretary's chair.

Mark, Jeff Corcoran, Gordon Metcalfe and a stenographer hastily deplaned from the Gulfstream aircraft into two waiting black Lincoln limousines and from there they moved quickly to the estate where Bobby Drew Houston was waiting.

Houston's Secret Service detail had already cleared the area and they were waiting at the gate to let the two limos through the heavy ornamental gates. The cars moved rapidly down the long flower lined driveway into the turnaround and after the 4 secret service people left the cars and looked around, the passengers were quickly moved through the massive doors into the foyer. Bobby Houston was waiting for them and greeted everyone with his most typical Texas bravado.

"Welcome everyone! Wish I could say to my humble little home, but this place is even over the top for a Texas politician!"

The newly arrived guests smiled politely and Mark responded, "Governor, thank you for agreeing to see us on such quick notice. We have some very important things to talk to you about and we would like to get to it right away if you don't mind."

Bobby responded, "Surely! Why don't we move out into the Sun Room – it has a right pretty view of the Gulf. Can I get you gentlemen and lady anything to drink?"

They all asked for iced tea, while Bobby settled on a double whiskey on the rocks. Mark began the meeting "Bobby, I don't really think that I have to tell you this, but I'm sure you know that you are in a whole lot of trouble after what you did with your Mayors a few days ago. I'm at a total loss to understand why you did what you did, but I'm not here to even try to find out. You did it, and it is your albatross to wear now.

"I know that you and your folks are making contact with a lot of members of the next session of the House, which means only one thing to me – and that is that you think you have an outside chance of getting elected IF the election gets thrown into the House. But let's just look at that for a minute. The new Attorney General has already taken you to the Grand Jury, and it is our understanding that he is within days if not hours of indicting you on a number of charges relating to vote tampering.

"Do you seriously think that those folks in the House would have any interest whatsoever in voting for someone who has just been indicted for any number of serious crimes? Really?"

"Well, General, don't you forget that I'm innocent until proven guilty. At least that's how I always understood our legal system.

But maybe you big time military boys operate by a different set of rules."

"Bobby, I'm not going to even pretend that I heard that arrogant slur - but of course 'innocent until proven guilty' is one of the basic fundamentals of our legal system that even your are entitled to. But surely you have to realize that is a very slim hope that you are clinging to. But, you know what, it really doesn't come down to someone having to prove you are either innocent or guilty. In the eyes of the people of the United States, my friend, you have already been convicted!"

"Well, now slow down General. That's easy for you to say, but I'm not so sure that that ass-hole John whats-his-name Marshall can prove any of this."

Gordon then finally spoke for the first time. "Bobby, I guess I am not totally surprised by your attitude so far, so let me get to the real point of this visit. We know all about the dealings surrounding Jimmy Foxworthy and why he so quickly withdrew from the campaign. It wasn't because you offered him the vice-presidency. It was because you illegally had pictures taken of him banging his bimbo blonde song leader. Believe it or not, someone on your staff has made those pictures available to us, and we know that Jimmy Foxworthy is ready to testify how you then blackmailed him into withdrawing. Now, do you want to deny this, Bobby?"

All at once Bobby Drew Houston turned completely ashen as he sunk back into his chair. He ran his hand through his hair before he was barely able to speak. "You guys aren't really going to make that stuff public, are you? My political career is probably already ruined, but that would ruin my family, my marriage. My God, you aren't really serious about this are you?"

Gordon answered, "Bobby, we are serious. Our Administration is not going to cover up crimes committed by high officials – either in our party or someone else's party. But before we release the details of what we know we would like to propose an honorable thing for you to do. Resign from the Governorship and in writing and by television appearance release all of your Electoral delegates to vote for whomever they think is most qualified to be President.

"Don't force those poor people to have to make a choice that will scare half of them to death. Give them their freedom and let them decide who they will vote for. We are not asking for your endorsement either. We just want them to have a choice.

Mark then interjected "But just so there is no misunderstanding, we *are* going to turn this information over to the Attorney General's office this Friday, and he can do what he wants with it. But once we take office we will pick up this case and prosecute it to the full extent of the law. We think that you did stupid and undoubtedly illegal things to try and get yourself elected President, and now you are going to have to pay for those actions. But at least you can do one honorable thing and release those Electors to vote their own consciences."

Bobby spoke up in almost a whisper. "I see that you have someone recording this whole conversation, so I guess you really are serious about this. It kind of reminds me of an old movie which was a real favorite of mine. You're making me an offer I can't refuse. That's it, isn't it?"

"That's it Bobby!"

Chapter 51

Early the following Tuesday morning, the networks all received an alert from the Headquarters of Governor Bobby Houston to be ready for an announcement from the Governor at 12 noon.

****

For once in the last few months all the leading talking heads were available for this performance, although it was safe to say that they were certainly not prepared for what might be coming. Houston had been remarkably quiet the last few weeks and most of the "informed" discussion related to how he was going to mount a workable defense as his date with the Grand Jury approached.

Greg Putnam opened their discussion as they waited for the noon appointed hour to arrive. "It is certainly not easy to predict what Houston plans to say today. He has certainly made it clear that he is in this race to the bitter end - and we know that he has been canvassing all of the delegates who are pledge to him in the last week or so, hoping to prevent any defections."

"That's right Greg, "Roger chimed in. "We also know that people from Worthington's camp have been calling on electors from both the President's party and Houston's as well."

"What are they promising these electors Roger? And if they are promising some real nice goodies, is that even legal - not to mention the morality of it!"

"Well, everything we hear, and frankly most of the electors we have talked to are very, very closed mouth about this, but up until a couple of days ago, they weren't promising anything. No jobs, no money, nada! They are saying simply: consider the candidates you are being asked to vote for, and follow your conscience - for the good of the United States of America - do what is right!"

"But then in the last day or so there has been a flurry of blog and tweeter stories, rumors at best, the offers to defect have been substantial."

"Any idea where those rumors are coming from?"

"No, but you know how it is - leak a nasty little rumor and it spreads like the Zika virus, so we'll just have to wait and see!"

Peter looked straight into the camera and in a very low, modulated voice said "Do you suppose that we might possibly be about to hear something refreshing from the mouth of a politician for a change? Is that even possible?"

****

With that the Governor of Texas began to speak:

"My fellow Americans, and especially all of you who voted for me in November and have supported me in Texas for so many years, I thank you. I thank you for that support. My staff and I have been in non- stop meetings the last few days looking at the different possibilities before us in the next few days. They are solidly behind me wanting to fight it out in the electoral college and if need be into the House of Representatives in January. You all know me as a fighter - never ducking a good fight - and hanging in there to the bitter end. But, and there is a big but here that we have to consider. Do we have the votes - both in the electoral college and in the House of Representatives to win this thing?

"Much to the disappointment of my staff, and my family, I have come to the inescapable conclusion that we do not have those votes, nor are we likely to come up with them in the next few days. So, I have concluded that the statesmanlike path to take is to clear the way for all of my electors to vote their conscience in the upcoming electoral college. With this decision made I am also submitting my resignation as Governor of Texas to the Attorney General of the State of Texas effective immediately.

It has been my pleasure and honor to have served all of you over these past many years, and I will miss you greatly. God Bless the great state of Texas, and God Bless the United States of America."

With that said, the camera went blank and the announcement was over.

****

The talking heads all sat still for a moment as the message sunk in. Greg Putnam looked at Henry and said "Henry?"

"Well! That was not what I was expecting, but then again, I wasn't at all sure just what I *was* expecting. No bravado, no puffed up opinion of himself. Actually a hint of humility, and a minimum of words. Was that really Bobby Houston? It certainly looked like him, and sounded like him - but was that really him?

Greg spoke next and said, "Whatever led up to this announcement, and I have to believe there was something else

258

going on that we will have to wait to hear - the result is certainly that freeing up his electors means Mark Worthington is undoubtedly going to be our next President. Houston only needs 8 or 10 votes to go his way and there are at least that many electors in Texas who will choose to vote for Worthington. Some will still vote for Houston, and none will swing to the President, so Mark Worthington is the big winner here!"

"Roger, do you have any doubts about the results of this bombshell?"

"None. My guess is that Worthington will get no less than 25 of those electors defecting to him, and that seals his win. But, the big question is 'why' did he do it?'

Chapter 52

The night before the Houston announcement the group of Senators widely known as the Mavericks were invited to Sen.Bob Madison's home. The group had already met in November when Madison had challenged them to join up with the Independents. The end result was not as good as Bob had hoped but he did manage to pick up a couple of recruits to join their small band of pioneers in the Senate. But the group was surprised to hear from Bob once again asking them to get together for breakfast.

The Senator from Wyoming asked "Bob, what's up with all of these maverick meetings? I really like you old boys – and girls" - with a courtly nod to Ellen Livingston, the only lady in the group – "But I can't be a meetin' every week. I don't know about the rest of you, but I'm up to my ass in committee meetings right now!"

"I know, I know! I called you together on behalf of Mark Worthington and his inner circle team. Gordon Metcalfe, here, has been appointed Chief of Staff for Mark and he has something he would like to propose. Gordon?"

With that Gordon stood and went to an easel placed between their two tables. "Senator Livingston – Gentlemen! Mark has asked me to speak to you this morning about the direction the country takes if he should manage to secure the Presidency by some means in the next month or so. We met yesterday and we came up with a very short list of items that we think are extremely important for the United States, and we would like you and your staff's help in crafting some meaningful legislation dealing with these issues.

"Mark and our small staff came up with a list of items that we think should move to the head of the line in priority."

With that Mark turned back the first blank page to show the six top priority initiatives:

1. Develop a humane and workable way to deal with the Immigration issue in our country

2. Find a long term fix to save Social Security for the next fifty years

3. Repairing the U.S. Health Care system to provide the widest net of coverage at the lowest possible cost to all Americans

4. Develop and fund a program to move the U.S. into the top 10 countries in the world with regard to Education for every child

5. Develop a program for the U.S. to deal with both Domestic and International Terrorism

6. Create a massive infrastructure improvement program for the entire U.S.

"Now, these aren't the only important issues the new administration will want to deal with, and we fully understand that. So what we are proposing to do is to zero in on as many of these issues as we can in the next six months.......

"yes yes. six months, not 100 days. We want to get a jump on the 'legislative deliberation' that needs to take place - it's you folks that can give us that leading edge....."

At this point several of the Senators all began to speak at once. They pointed out some other very important issues such as what to do about Roe v. Wade; gay rights issues; the national debt, the role of the U.S. in the world, defense spending, gun control; rewriting the tax code, and several more that came spilling out over the course of the next hour or so.

At this point Ellen spoke up. "Why don't we let Gordon finish his presentation and let's see what Mark Worthington wants us to do – how 'bout it?"

One final question was asked "What's with this first 6 months plan Gordon? Whatever happened to the first 100 days?"

Gordon quickly regained control of the conversation, and began with a quick explanation of the six month idea. "We simply do not want to get in a position where we are seen to be cramming legislation down the throats of the American people – and also the Congress I might add. We think there are all too many examples of hastily written legislation that has come back to bite everyone in the behind because of the need to get it done in the first hundred days. There is nothing magical about 100 days, now is there?"

On that Gordon received general agreement. "So, we take our time on a limited agenda of issues and come up with some really good, constitutionally sound laws that will stand up to Supreme Court scrutiny and will greatly improve how things are done!"

Another one of the Mavericks ventured "That's a novel approach and I think one that has been long overdue. I commend you and General Worthington for this idea. But, what do you want from us?"

"Ah, I thought you would never ask! We would like you to assign some of your staff to just one of these priority issues, and perhaps 2-3 of the additional ideas, and have them draw up a white paper that would capture what you think needs to be done, upsides and downsides, how much it will cost, or conversely save, the likelihood of getting it passed in both houses, and whether it can be completed in the first six months. Bullet points, and graphs, showing assumptions, and probably conclusions.

"Folks, here's your chance to help break the log jam in Congress by coming up with some real bi-partisan ideas. We want to present these programs not as Republican, or Democrat or Independence issues, but as American issues. These are issues that are crying out for meaningful reform legislation, and that is what we are aiming to achieve. Will you help us?"

One by one the 10 Senators present rose to their feet and agreed to take one of the issues as their project. Once the top 6 listed were called for the remaining 4 Senators picked up one of the other issues that Gordon had mentioned.

****

Gordon got in a cab and hurried back to the Willard to report to Mark that his meeting with the Mavericks had been an enormously successful venture. But, he then said, I think it is time we book you for a prime time speech about what is going on right now as far as the Presidential process goes. Mark was in total agreement and they agreed to meet with a couple of speechwriters later that evening to put something meaningful together.

Chapter 53

Ellen Livingston had total respect for Mark Worthington and that respect began from the first day she met him out on the primary trail. She was a solid member of the Senate and deeply respected by all of her peers including those on the opposite side of the aisle. She was now on her way to meet with the man who probably was going to be the next President of the United States, and she couldn't help but think of her thoughts on that first meeting.

From the minute he began to talk during the very first debate, she felt that she would be honored to step aside and let him run all the way to the White House. She admired his positions, the powerful but understated delivery of his message and his deft handling of both the reporter's questions and the jabs of the other contenders. All she could think of was how 'presidential' he seemed to be. There was no one thing. He wasn't stuffy, or overbearing. He was the kind of person you would just love to sit down with at the corner Starbucks. He always looked right at you, and you knew he was listening to you – and he never interrupted you in mid sentence. He could disagree with you and not make you feel angry. He was always courteous to all of the candidates, never demeaning nor belittling, and as far as she could determine he was never caught in a lie - big or small! And here she was about to meet him for what reason? Well, she would soon know.

****

As Ellen entered the meeting room Mark quickly rose to his feet and approached her with a big smile, taking both of her hands in his. "Ellen, it is so good to see you again! It's been a tough few weeks hasn't it?"

"Well, let's just say, it has certainly been interesting! How has Janet held up?"

"Tired, but just fine. Thank you for asking. But please sit down. I ordered some fresh coffee, can I pour you a cup?"

With the pleasantries out of the way, Mark quickly moved to the reason he had asked Ellen to meet. "Ellen, we have been going over a lot of things the last couple of weeks, but mostly we have been talking about people for key jobs in the new administration."

Then Mark caught himself and he laughed softly, saying "That is of course if we can finally get this thing wrapped up and we actually win. Don't want to get too far ahead of myself here."

Ellen said "I truly think it is going to be settled very soon now and like they say, I think "You're the Man!"

"Thank you Ellen, I hope you are right. But more to the point, as I indicated earlier I asked you to come in today because I want to offer you a key position in our administration. As a matter of fact this is the first position I want to fill. I want you to be the next Secretary of State. How about it?"

Ellen had had some dramatic experiences in her life, including her marriage and then her very traumatic divorce, followed by a couple of runs for the United States Senate, but she never felt a thump in her chest like she had just experienced. Secretary of State? Oh, my God, he is not kidding. He just offered me the opportunity to be the Secretary of State. She suddenly realized that her eyes were closed and she had stopped breathing – did I just have a heart attack? Oh, my God, Secretary of State! All of these emotions in about 5 seconds, when she finally spoke.

"Mr. President, I am truly humbled by your offer, and I would be proud to serve as Secretary of State in your administration. Thank you so much for your confidence in me…thank you so much!"

"Great, great! I have to tell you we really wrestled with this because we knew that we were going to give up a very valuable asset in the Senate if you elected to take this job, but I felt so strongly that you were just exactly the right person that I told our team I'll take the loss of you not being in the Senate for the tremendous gain I will get with you at the State Department and sitting with me in Cabinet meetings. And I just can't tell you how pleased I am that you accepted!"

"Again, Mr. President, I am truly humbled. Thank you so much!"

****

When Ellen finally made it to the sidewalk in front of Mark's Hotel, she looked around until she found a place to sit down, and pulling out her I Phone she called Bob Madison in his office. His secretary put her through immediately and she got right to the point. "Bob, will you take me to dinner tonight? We need to talk about some very important things. Please don't ask right now, but can you pick me up at 7?"

He readily agreed and she placed the phone back in her purse and thought to herself, "I was just offered the most important position in the Cabinet of the President of the United States, and my first thought was to call Bob Madison – and that's because I am deeply in love with him! I have slept with him, but have I ever really told him just how much I love him? Have I told him that I want to marry him, and live the rest of my life with him? Can we make this work if I am at State and traveling all over the world while he is working his brains out in the Senate? Well, damn it why not? We're entitled to have a life outside the office, aren't we? Oh, my God, I can hardly wait till 7 o'clock, I want to have him hold me and tell me he loves me and yes, of course, we can make it work. Oh, my God, Secretary of State!"

****

Bob arrived promptly at 7 and Ellen opened the door and before he could even move into the room she threw her arms around him and kissed him with a deep and penetrating kiss. She then whispered to him "I love you Bob Madison. Do you have any idea how much I love you? I really want to spend the rest of my life doing exactly what we are doing right now, hugging each other and kissing real kisses."

Bob gently pushed back a few inches and said, I love you too, Ellen, and I want to spend the rest of my life with you as well. Can we go somewhere this weekend and get married?"

She looked up at him and the tears began to flow down her cheeks and she said, "Secretary of State Bob. Secretary of State!"

He drew her close to him again, and whispered in her ear, "Then we better get married this weekend, because who knows when we will have the time later on. So it is Secretary of State. Damn I knew Mark Worthington was smart, but I didn't know he was that smart – to pick you for State? So now, I get to pick you as Mrs. Robert Madison. I guess that makes me at least the second smartest guy in the United States tonight!"

He then reached in his pocket and took out a handkerchief and wiped the tears from her cheeks, and once again repeated, "Yes, Ellen Livingston, I do love you more than anything in the world and I do want you to be my wife for evermore! Now let's go get something to eat and celebrate! And then we can make some plans for this weekend!"

****

Bob Madison and Ellen Livingston, long accepted as a 'power couple' in Washington secured a marriage license and booked a suite in a toney hotel far out on Long Island Sound. They invited their children and grandchildren and a few friends from their past as well as around ten Senators and their wives. It made for a nice wedding party - not too large - not too small, and before a minister they both had known for a long time, they exchanged vows, and rings and pledge to love each other for ever!

And believe it or not, somehow this event was pulled off with only one reporter and attendance photographer (both invited) present. Sometimes miracles do happen!

Chapter 54

The President was in his office but he wasn't sitting behind the big desk. He was pacing back and forth and his Chief of Staff worried that he might actually wear a path on the beautiful rug that was at the center of the room. His Chief of Staff, Attorney General John Marshall and his chief political advisor all sat calmly in the wingback chairs waiting for his motor to run down.

"We can still win this thing, I know we can. Can't we?"

Martin Remington was the first to offer an opinion. "Mr. President, the odds are pretty long, but yes, you can still win the election."

"See, I knew it! That's what I have been telling all these yo-yos around here for weeks. "

"But," Remington continued as if he hadn't even heard what the President had just said, "the time is getting very short and the odds are very long – very long!"

"Okay, okay, but what do we have to do to make it happen? . I have never wanted anything so bad in my life and once I get sworn in, there will be a lot of people around this town who will wish they had done a whole lot more to get me elected. There will be a blood bath like this town has never seen – believe me, a blood bath. I'm going to chop the balls off thousands of these blood suckers who didn't get behind me all the way!"

John Sylvester Marshall, the newly appointed interim Attorney General finally caught an opportunity to speak. "Mr. President why don't you shut up and sit down!"

The President did stop pacing and the blood seemed to drain completely from his face, and his mouth dropped open, but no sound came out. He felt like he had been slapped hard right across the face and for once in his life he was totally without words. So he turned and went behind his desk and sat down as he had just been directed.

Marshall continued, "Look, I think it is safe to say that I did manage to keep you from getting impeached a few days ago, and maybe I even kept you from being indicted and thrown in jail. So, now, it is time for you to shut up and listen to us for a change."

The President stammered "Look, you can't talk to me like that….I'm the President…."

Marshall interrupted with "You are barely the President of anything anymore. Whether you like it or not, you are an accidental President and with that big, uncontrollable mouth of yours you nearly brought down this entire administration. You very nearly got yourself thrown bodily out of here and perhaps even thrown so far as Leavenworth. So it's time you shut up and listen while we try to salvage something out of this goddamn mess you have made."

The Chief of Staff was so stunned by all of this that he sat perfectly rigid in his chair and didn't even think of making any kind of comment. All he could think of was how close this seemed to be to a coup. The only thing missing was the silver bullet to the back of the President's head.

Remington spoke up with "It's over. Do you understand that statement? It is over. You don't have a prayer in the Electoral College, so if either of the other two can work a little magic there, then it is over right there. And frankly, we know that

Worthington's people have been contacting a lot of the damn few votes we do have and we suspect that a lot of them will cave and change their vote to Worthington. But on the off chance that we can get by that little get together, we have been in touch with all of our representatives in the House – just in case there might be a chance that we get that far.

"But please remember the Republicans have the most votes in the House, and the Independents have a large number as well. But to let you know just how popular you really are, fully 70% of the Democrats – Democrats mind you – the people elected by your party that we talked to said there was no way in Hell they were going to vote for you if it came down to a vote in the House.

"So now, your Royal Arrogance, that is why John just got through telling you to shut up and sit down! You are through and the only thing we and you can do at this time is try and get you out of this office without a ticket to Leavenworth, and perhaps salvage a tiny little bit of your badly damaged reputation! Do you understand what we are telling you?"

The President sat slumped over with his hands on the desk and he slowly raised his head and said, "I understand. So what do we do now?"

Marshall spoke up and said "We keep you out of sight as much as possible, and just work on damage control. Right now it isn't so much the damage to your own image that we are worried about as it is the real damage to the Democratic Party. To have a President impeached or indicted for various crimes could set this party back for 10 years - maybe more.. And with a guy about to come into this office who is squeaky clean and riding a huge wave of public support, our party can't afford a ten year set back. We will let you know when we want you to speak on any issue, and when you do, you will read what we write for you. You will not make yourself available for any off the cuff press conferences and absolutely no tweets. Is that clearly understood?"

The President nodded yes, and the three men rose and left the Oval Office and a completely shattered and broken President sitting at his desk sobbing uncontrollably.

Chapter 55

With the date for the electors to gather and cast their votes bearing down on everyone, the newspapers, magazines, television news channels and hundreds of blogs were consumed with the political situation facing the country. But actually the facts were pretty clear: no candidate had the requisite 270 electoral votes to claim victory in the election. Oh, yes, Mark Worthington had clearly won the popular votes but so had Al Gore and Hillary Clinton, and ultimately they lost their election bids.

But complicating the situation even more was the impending indictments of both Governor Bobby Houston and the totally murky situation surrounding the President and his possible voter fraud. Only General Mark Worthington was left standing tall and untainted (at least as far as anyone could determine.)

Then the totally unexpected and almost unthinkable happened.

****

All of the News channels, papers and other media were alerted to yet another hastily called press conference. This time it was the White House asking for prime time - for an important message from the President of the United States.

****

Seated alone in the Oval Office the President of the United States faced an imposing array of both Domestic and International microphones. As the camera zeroed in it was obvious that all this controversy had taken an enormous toll on the President. He was drawn and his familiar booming voice seemed to coming from a very deep and hollow canyon.

"My fellow Americans, I come before you tonight to acknowledge a couple of very difficult facts of life. Simply stated I have to acknowledge to you that we trailed badly in the popular vote in the recent election. But even more devastating is the fact that we also did very poorly in counting Electoral votes. Unlike Governor Houston, and despite all that is going on, I am still the President of the United States, and I will remain President until January 20th.

"I remind everyone that despite the gloom which seems to surround our presidential fortunes at the moment that we Democrats do control a very large bloc of votes in the House of Representatives in Congress, and if this election goes into the House we are in a very strong position to still pull off an unprecedented and unexpected victory.

"However, I do not want to belabor what is obviously a tenuous position. So, therefore I must also be realistic. So, to all of my victorious electors and also the Democrats in the House, I release them to vote as their conscience dictates. Of course, I would hope that they would stick with me and the Democratic Party in these very difficult days coming up. We are entering a period of considerable uncertainty, and it just won't be in the best interest of the country to prolong the agony this election process poses.

"So, I offer my congratulations to Gen. Worthington for what appears to be his inevitable victory. I am truly sorry that we did not do a better job pushing our agenda, but it is what it is.

"Good night to you all and may God Bless America."

****

The talking heads were quick to speak up after this most unexpected announcement from the President.

"Well, I'll be damned, if you will excuse my language" said Peter. "I cannot believe that he wrote that message, but whoever did write it had it right. He doesn't have a prayer and there is not much sense in prolonging the agony..."

Roger than added "No, no sense at all. But this is not a humble man, as we all know. He is a street fighter, and for him to take to national television to release the few electors he actually had, ,had to give him about the worst case of stomach anxiety as he has ever suffered.."

Finally Peter had to sum it up. "Well, we have probably seen one of the few times in this man's political career where he listened to his advisors and acted accordingly. Thought I would never see that!"

Chapter 56

December 5th was destined to be a very important day this year in the United States of America. Today was the day the Electors around the country gathered in their state capitol cities to cast their votes for the President and Vice President. In most Presidential election years this is not a particularly momentous occasion. The Electors gather and exchange greetings with their fellow electors, fill out the required number of ballots, state who they are voting for and adjourn for lunch at some high end restaurant (of course all paid for by their political party.)

About half of our 50 states require that the electors of the political party that wins the popular vote in their state cast their vote for the candidate that carried their state. But then there are the other half of the states that don't mandate that the electors follow the election returns. But even in these states the pressure to cast their vote for the candidate who carried the state is so great that precious few electors have the guts to a) risk the wrath of their political parties and/or b)take the chance that someone will file a lawsuit challenging their changed vote.

So it would seem the electoral college is just an exercise in total futility. But then along comes a year like this one where no one of the three leading contenders won a majority of the Electoral votes. But our founding fathers had a solution for even that eventuality: if no candidate won a majority of the electoral votes, the election would go to the House of Representatives where each state's delegation would vote as one. One vote per state. The candidate who wins 26 states is then elected President.

But this wasn't any ordinary, run of the mill election. This year the electors who should have voted for the President (and that was a precious few as it turned out) had to swallow hard and cast their vote for a man who was on the verge of being impeached and perhaps indicted for the crime of attempting to tamper with the election process in Illinois (one of the few states that he actually did carry.)

Then the candidate who actually ran second in the three man race and who did accumulate a sizable number of electoral votes also tried to tamper with the votes in Texas (a state that he also did carry) and for that little indiscretion he is facing a grand jury investigation, possible impeachment as Governor and potential jail time. Now just what kind of decision do these 200 or so electors face when they consider marking their electoral ballots? Do they want to vote for a man that quite possibly is going to jail for his illegal activities? Is that the kind of person they really want sitting in the White House? What to do?

Representatives of Mark Worthington understood all of this and their efforts were successful in contacting nearly all of the electors nominally pledged to Houston and to the President. They only reached out to those states that did not mandate automatic votes for the winners. At Mark Worthington's explicit instructions they offered nothing to these electors should they decide to switch their vote. They merely pointed out that the electors had the right to change their vote should their conscience so dictate. The contacts were all made by Bryce Randolph, so Mark knew that his "no promises" instructions would be followed with no deviation. It was obvious to all concerned that a great many electors were facing a very serious personal dilemma.

The news media was speculating every day as to what would happen – indeed what should happen. But, of course, the decision was up to a handful of individuals around the country. And so on the morning of December 5th, several leading newspapers and several news magazines had headlines reading along this line:

WHAT WILL THE ELECTORS DO?

One by one the electors entered their respective capitols and faced the minute when they were called upon to declare who they were voting for – for you see this is not a secret ballot. The elector must publicly declare the candidate he is voting for.

And thus the votes were cast.

****

Chapter 57

The news began breaking across the United States starting of course in the Eastern Time Zone. All of the major news networks broke into their scheduled broadcasts with bulletins. The talking heads were all gathered in anticipation of something monumental happening.

Richard spoke first. "Ladies and gentlemen we are interrupting what you normally watch at this time for some extremely important news regarding the Presidential election. Electors have begun casting their votes around the country and beginning in the Eastern time zone, an incredible and nearly unthinkable event is occurring. One after another, electors who were supposed to vote for either the President of the United States, or the Republican candidate, Governor Bobby Houston, of Texas, are declaring that they are voting for General Mark Worthington, the Independence Party candidate."

Greg Putnam, the network anchor added, "because we knew that there was the possibility of some defections among the electors our network has positioned reporters at every state capitol to record whatever might happen today. And in what now appears to be an unprecedented movement, electors who had the right to change their vote have stepped up and declared their right to change their vote from either the President or Governor Houston to Mark Worthington, simply because their conscience would not allow them to vote for either Houston or the President."

Richard added, "Unprecedented is hardly the word for what is happening today. There have been defections in the past, when one or two electors bucked the general rules, and those few votes had absolutely no impact on the final result of the particular election. But what we are seeing today is akin to the tide rising to the point of flowing over the breakwater walls. Peter, as our resident Democratic Party analyst what do you make of this?"

"Well, Richard, the President had gathered so few electoral votes – something like 31? – that it really doesn't surprise me that he is losing a good part of even those few. His address to the country releasing his electors was seen by some as the statesmanlike thing to do, but it was really locking the barn door after all the horses had already fled. Our reports out of the White House indicate that the President has practically disappeared from sight. All communication from the oval office seems to be coming from either John Sylvester Marshall, the interim Attorney General or Martin Remington, his closest political advisor – and frankly it isn't much at all. It appears that the President took his licking at the polls very personally and we all know what a proud individual he is and all the talk of impeachment and indictments has to be weighing heavily on him. However none of the defecting Democrats has indicated that the President released them from their "commitment" but that they simply say they could not vote for him in good conscience."

Henry, the well known Republican analyst then spoke up saying "That is almost the same thing we are hearing from the Republican electors Peter. Yes, they had officially been released by Governor Houston but practically to a person they have said that they simply could not in good conscience have cast a vote for Governor Houston to be the next President."

"Thank you Henry. What seems to have taken hold today is like a dark and stormy raincloud lifting from all over the United

States and in a moment of genuine solidarity a great many people in our country decided to put their conscience ahead of their party loyalties."

Greg Putnam then turned to Richard and said "Richard, that was a beautiful way of saying something like a miracle happened in our country today. A relatively small group of people who as fate would have it were placed in a position to do the "Right Thing" – and they did it! In the rancorous atmosphere of today's political landscape, for this small group of people to actually stand up and say "Enough" is really something of a miracle. It's hard to tell how long this " period of enlightenment" will last. As cynical analysts, all of us know that the honeymoon probably won't last very long, but thank God for these people who truly saw an opportunity to do the right thing – and they did it. God love them all!"

Chapter 58

December 6th

Newspapers all over the United States and around the World as well on the day after the electors cast their ballots could hardly contain themselves in their praise for the 169 Electors who stood up and abandoned their party to cast their electoral vote for Mark Worthington

The final electoral vote count now stood as follows:

Mark Worthington: 430 (with 270 needed to win)

The President: 15

Bobby Houston: 90

The Television analysts from all the major networks, CNN and Fox and anyone else who carried the news worldwide all officially declared Mark Worthington the winner, and now President-elect of the United States. Everyone now waited for a message from the new President-elect.

****

Early in the morning of December 6th all of the pertinent networks were notified that Mark Worthington would be addressing the citizens of the United States at 8pm(est)

regarding the sudden and stunning end of the controversy surrounding this year's election.

At precisely 8pm Mark Worthington stepped in front of a bank of microphones in the ballroom of the Willard Hotel in Washington and addressed the people of the United States.

"My fellow Americans I come before you this evening with great pride and joy in my heart for the brave men and women who yesterday chose what they considered to be the honorable course of action with regard to their electoral ballots. We had hoped that at least 9 of these electors would be moved to take that action which would be all that we needed to get over the top. But when the final tally was made there were 169 men and women who were brave enough to vote with their hearts in this extraordinarily important exercise in our Democracy. I cannot praise them enough nor can I thank them adequately. I can only hope that I will live up to their trust in me and serve them honestly and faithfully.

"I have spoken to both the President and to Governor Houston by phone this afternoon, and they have graciously accepted the results of the Electoral balloting. I must add that they both reminded me that they and their parties continue to have substantial support in the Congress, but I truly hope that we can work together for all of the citizens of this great country.

 It has not been easy for either of them since election day, and I pray that you will be cautious in your assessment of their recent behavior until the justice system has a chance to work as it is designed to do.

"But now I would like to turn to the very serious matter of how we are going to govern in the days ahead. We are about to move into a period of unprecedented opportunity, but also unprecedented difficulty as well. As you all know my political party is very small compared to the two older established parties. We will have less than 100 dedicated representatives and senators in the incoming Congress. Our new administration will have to depend on both of these two grand old parties being willing to join us and work with us as we tackle the great and pressing issues facing our country. Actually, I might add that neither of them will be able to get their way in Congress without our support either. With all due humility I am asking the leaders of both of them to set aside the seemingly insurmountable differences between us and work with us on an agenda that can result in good things for our country.

"The Independence Party itself is a direct consequence of the millions of voters in this country who grew tired of the intransigence of the Liberals on the Left and the Conservative die-hards on the right being unable to set aside their rigid party lines and find common ground in solving all of these knotty problems. My career was in the military, and I can tell you with absolute certainty that in a difficult, combat situation, you have to rely on the people on your right - and on your left, because your life depends on that trust. And that is exactly what we will be doing as we move into January!

"The facts were that that these millions of voters were looking for something in between the two poles - some leadership that would be based on practical, common sense approaches to problems.

"So here we are. Neither of the older parties has enough votes to force either of their agendas into law. And now, the Presidency belongs to the new Independence Party - the Common Sense Party! Can we make this work? Of course we can - and we will make it work!

"I am counting on the emergence of a new type of leadership - statesmen, if you will, who will be willing to work hard, accepting compromise gracefully, and crafting legislation that will better the lives of all of our citizens. That my fellow citizens is the challenge we will set before the new Congress in January!

"In the meantime I am setting a timetable of six months from inauguration day to propose, debate and define what has to be done with regard to six major issues.

"We must develop a humane and workable way to deal with the Immigration issue in our country;

"We have to arrive at a long term fix to save Social Security for today's Seniors and for all of those in our country counting on those benefits for at least the next fifty years;

"We must redesign and repair the U.S. Health Care system to provide the widest net of coverage at the lowest possible cost for all Americans:

"We must harness all of the great minds in our country to develop and fund a program to move the USA, once and for all, into the top 10 countries in the world with regard to Education for every one of our children;

"W e must create a humane but effective means to deal with Domestic and International terrorism;

"And finally, the time has come to launch a massive infrastructure improvement program for the entire United States. The world's greatest industrial and technological country cannot be satisfied with a 75 year old frayed and decaying infrastructure.

"I am absolutely aware that there are many other extremely important and pressing issues that will ultimately have to be dealt with: such as our responsibility with regard to the rest of the world; the issues surrounding human rights in this country as well as elsewhere in the world; the role our military should play in the world; how to guarantee our citizens clean air and a clean and abundant supply of water; and finally of great importance is what we have to do to be able to finance any or all of these great projects.

"These and many other pressing concerns will be addressed in time, but only after we have dealt with the first six. It will be my goal as perhaps never before to focus the White House, my party and hopefully all of the rest of the incoming Congress on finding workable solutions to these problems.

"Starting today the name of the game in Washington will be 'hard work' and serious deliberation from all three parties on each and every issue. The White House will not be issuing directives, but will expect the Congress to debate the serious implications of each of these issues, and then after thoughtful and unharried deliberation, they will come up with legislation that the White House, the three major political parties, the Supreme Court and most of all the citizens of the United States can be proud of.

"I promise you that my Cabinet and I will be doing everything in our power to set an example of hard work, coupled with good old fashioned Common Sense!

"Finally, I want to announce that I have offered three distinguished public servants positions in my new Cabinet, of course subject to Senate approval. But I am sure that you will be as pleased as I am to know that first of all Senator Ellen

Livingston of New Jersey has accepted my request to become the next Secretary of State of the United States. She is very smart, experienced and highly qualified to held this vital position.

"Secondly, Aaron Freedman, the former Attorney General of the United States has agreed to become Attorney General in my administration. He has demonstrated great skill and immense courage in performing these same duties in the previous administrations and I am delighted to him join our team.

"And finally Governor Earl Potts of Iowa has accepted an appointment as the next Secretary of Agriculture. He has tremendous experience representing a great farm state and has been a trusted advisor for the last several months. I am delighted to have him accept this appointment.

"Please join me in welcoming these three fine people into my administration.

"In conclusion tonight, let me ask you to join me in my effort to bring a more civil tone to the politics of our nation. We can all continue to be passionate about our positions, because passion is what drives successful people and successful movements. But, let's also be aware that some of our neighbors may not share our passion, and that is every bit their right. Let's all try to listen to each other, trying to understand what those neighbors are thinking about on the issues. Then let's try to see how we might find a path through all of these conflicting passions, to an acceptable and honorable solution. To me, that is what Democracy is all about.

"I ask for your prayers and your patience as we move on to the work of our country in the months and years ahead. God bless all of you, and God bless the United States of America!"

Epilogue

On January 19th, John Black was asked to appear on the NBC morning show to talk about his new book on the making of a President. " I have interviewed all of the principle players in this year's election and I have come to one important and inescapable conclusion: What happened in this Election was inevitable. The Independents were bound to prevail at some point in time.

"But now the real challenge is finding a way to make three large political parties work together in a productive way. The English have been doing it for centuries. But this is going to be a very new experience for the United States.

"Indeed, for all those men and women we have just called to Washington, a new dawn is breaking!"

Acknowledgements

It's my great pleasure to acknowledge several people who have contributed significantly in the final creation of this book.

My Son-in-law Don Mulkey took my sketchy description and was able to come up with exactly the right concept for the cover - my deepest thanks to him!

A also want to thank Melissa Stoneman of Moore Graphics for all of the help and support she has provided with this and my two previous publications. She has also been totally supportive of all my students in the publication of their autobiographies - well over 20 of the 28 books completed so far. Her friendly, helpful and always understanding attitude are certainly appreciated by all of us.

I would also like to acknowledge the patience and understanding of my wife Caroline who has learned more about the idea of a 3rd major political party than she ever wanted to know.

I would also like to recognize Bob Miller, my fellow PORA Board member who provided just the right amount of positive feedback to me regarding my first political novel, ***The Inner Circle, a Modern Political Novel,*** and then expressing a desire to 'read' the sequel. So, Bob, here it is!

Finally, a big thanks to the two major political parties and our current President for their consistent lack of ability to focus on the real issues facing our country. The lack of leadership from both sides of the aisle has made it abundantly clear that it is time for a real change in our political structure - offering up abundantly fertile ground for even novice novelists like me!

About the Author

Dave Poling continues to live in Sun City West, Arizona with Caroline his wife of 56 years, and his ever present dog Sir Aston. He is active on the Board of the Property Owners and Residents Association (PORA) of Sun City West where he serves as Vice President. He continues to be responsible for the highly successful Adult Learning Program where he teaches ***How to Write Your Autobiography*** in Sun City West, as well as in Sun City Grand..

As much as he has enjoyed writing and publishing his own ***Autobiography*** and now his second novel, he considers the 29 autobiography books published by his students to be his real legacy.